I0012442

LATEST GUIDE

By TAGE BIRK

Copyright © 2023 Tage Birk

All rights reserved.

TABLE OF CONTENTS

TIPS AND TRICKS

How to Track Specific Quests

Between Main Story Quests with multiple Acts, Priority Quests, local Events and the many Side Quests you'll find all over, it can be hard to figure out where you need to go next and what you need to do. The tools you need to find quests are hidden on the map, but you just have to know where to look.

- Open your Map and use "Q" or the left D-Pad button to bring up the quest menu.
- Select the quest you want to track and press "Track" or "Untrack."
- If you zoom out on the map, you can see where the location is.

When Can You Get a Mount

As soon as you finish the Prologue tutorial and get to the main city of Kyovashad, you go to the stables where lorath bought a horse, but you can't buy one there either. Even if you bought a special edition of the game or bought cosmetics from the in-game store, you won't be able to have your own mount just yet.

Instead, you'll need to spend a lot of time moving through the Main Story's many Acts. You can do Acts 1, 2, and 3 in any order you want, but you have to finish all of them before you can start Act 4. When you finish the second main mission, "A Master's Touch," you'll finally be able to go to the stable and get your own horse.

Mounts in Diablo 4 let you move through large, open areas much faster, and you can customise them with different cosmetics that you can either unlock in the game or buy as microtransactions. You can't really attack while you're mounted, but you can use a special move that lets you jump into battle.

Always Open "Caches" to Gain Materials

You can get Caches of items by completing quests, opening certain chests, and even killing some monsters. You must click on these caches in your inventory to open them. If you don't, they will just sit there. When you click on the things on the ground, you can pick them up. Monsters will also drop other kinds of caches, which you will have to open from your inventory. There are different kinds of them:

- herb Caches hold herbs that can be used to make potions at the Alchemist.

- Potion Caches hold potions that boost your stats and the amount of experience you gain.

- Salvage Caches often have the rare materials needed to make or improve legendary weapons.

HOW TO DECIDE WHAT TO SALVAGE AT THE BLACKSMITH

The materials you get from salvaging items of different rarities are very important for levelling, crafting, and improving your gear, as well as for endgame content. If you're just starting out and want to know which reserves to build up first, you should definitely start filling your pockets with the magical materials you get when you destroy your gear at the blacksmith in town.

- look through your inventory and figure out what you can do to make your gear better. This is easy to do by comparing the gear in your inventory with what your character is already wearing. If the item is highlighted in green, it is better than what you already have equipped, and you should think about switching it out.

- Once you've put on any upgraded gear, talk to the Blacksmith in town and open the first tab, "Salvage."

- Click Common and Accept first, then Magic, and then Rare. Any materials that have been Salvaged will show up in the Blacksmith's menu, in the Salvage menu box on the lower left.

If you can't use something, try to save it. Also, when you salvage something, you can use the Wardrobe to give it a new "skin," or look. This is a very fancy mechanic that lets you change your armour and add an image on top of it. This was called "Enchanting" in Diablo 3, but in Diablo 4, it is called "Transmog."

But if you don't have enough Gold to buy certain items or services, you might want to sell your Common and Magic items instead and save Salvaging for Rare and then legendary items.

HOW GEMS AND SOCKETS WORK

Once you reach level 15, you'll start finding different kinds of gems that look like regular items but have a very specific use.

You'll also start to find different kinds of gear with one or two sockets where you can put the gems you find to get certain bonuses, depending on the type of gear you're putting the gem in. Even though you'll start to find more gems than you have sockets for (especially when opening up ore veins), they're still worth keeping.

Once you reach higher levels, you can talk to the Jeweller in town to start upgrading a gem with multiples of the same type to make a higher-quality gem of the same type. You'll also be able to take gems out of gear you've already put them in for a fee. This is useful if you find new gear and want to put the gems in it, or if you want to upgrade the gear they're in.

BUILDING YOUR CODEX OF POWER

The Codex is basically a list of legendary Aspects, which are added abilities that are part of a legendary item. These Aspects can be imprinted onto a Rare item to turn it into a legendary item. These Aspects are special because you can get them as rewards for completing dungeons. Each dungeon has a different Aspect, usually for a specific class, and you can use them to imprint on as many of your items as you want, as long as you have the upgrade materials.

You can also get the Aspect of a legendary Item from the Occultist. This Aspect will be stored in your inventory as a one-time-use item that you can imprint onto another piece of gear.

DIFFICULTY CAN BE CHANGED AT WORLD TIER STATUES

Your current World Tier affects how hard Diablo 4 is overall. You can change your World Tier at any time from the Character Select Screen or the World Tier Statue in Kyovashad. This makes the game harder and changes how characters die and how hard it is to fight in general.

If you change your World Tier, all active portals will close, all incomplete Whispers will start over, and any active Nightmare Dungeons (only available in Nightmare mode) will close.

WEAPONS DEGRADE WHEN YOU DIE

In Sanctuary, dying isn't too bad (unless you're playing on hardcore mode or higher). But you should know that every time your character dies, their weapons and armour get a little worse.

If your weapons or armour are broken, you should go to the Blacksmith, who will fix it for you.

REFUNDING YOUR SKILL TREE

Up to level 15, the Diablo 4 skill tree is kind enough to let players reset their entire skill tree for a small fee. It's an easy way to figure out what works for you and your style of play, or to take advantage of an opponent's weaknesses by making a few quick changes.

After level 15, it will cost more to make changes to the skill tree. luckily, the price isn't too high, and gold is easy to find in Sanctuary.

STUFF THAT WILL CARRY OVER ON A NEW CHARACTER

Since you can make more than one character on a server, it may seem hard to start over every time you play a different Class. There are a lot of things that can be shared with your other characters, no matter when you create them.

Some parts that are the same or stay the same are:

- Mount Skins were bought.

- lilith's shrines

- Earned money

- Codex is used at the local occultist

- Crafting materials (you can find this information on your character page by clicking "Materials & Stats" and then "Treasure Chest").

As you earn Renown in each region of the game, you can get rewards that help both your current Character and other Characters you make.

༺WALKTHROUGH༻

PROLOGUE: WANDERING

Dusk on the Mountain

After the exciting opening cutscene and making your character, you'll be thrown right into the world of Sanctuary. If you're still not sure what to do, check out our Classes guide.

Your journey starts in a snowy area of Sanctuary called Fractured Peaks. When you wake up in the cave, you'll need to find a safe place to stay because the storm is getting worse. Open your map and look for the gold symbol shown below to find where you need to go.

This is a nearby town where you can find safety. Follow the map in the top right corner and start going down the mountain. On the way down, you'll run into some Wargs. This is when you'll learn how to fight and avoid being hit.

If you keep going down the path, you'll find more enemies to fight and some things to smash for loot! Then go through the gates into Nevesk, a small town that has been left to die. here, you can hear the voice of a stranger calling out. Follow the voice to a house on the left and go through the door.

Inside, you'll meet Oswen, Vani, and a man who is babbling about demons coming out of the ruins. Vani says she will tell you everything, so follow her outside to a small tavern where you can talk with other villagers about where you are and what's going on. You can also find Isbel, who sells armor, and Stanis, who is a healer.

Vani will ask if you can protect them from whatever is out there, and now it's your turn to go explore the ruins.

Darkness Within

Go to Icehowl Ruins, which is a Dungeon on your map just north of the town

Along the way, you'll fight many different kinds of new enemies. When you get to the gate, go inside the Icehowl Ruins.

This will be your first time in a Diablo 4 Dungeon. Go out the back door and through the next door on the right to start your journey. Continue going through these doors until you get to a place with two doors. The one to your right is empty, but the one in front of you is full of enemies waiting to attack, so move forward to deal with them.

Keep going through these rooms until you see glowing doors on the right that you can go through. You can use a healing Well in this area.

If you keep walking down the hall, you'll reach the hell-Touched Corridors.

If you go right when you first start to look around, you'll find enemies ready to attack. After you've dealt with them, go into the next rooms to the left. here, more enemies are ready to fight you.

Take them out, then move forward into a bigger room with more enemies to fight.

Now, go through the door on the right side of the room to get to another area with more enemies to fight. Go through the door in the back of this room to find another healing Well, and then follow the path past it.

This will take you to a room where a headless priest is lying on the floor. Uh oh. When you talk to him, the boss fight with X'Fal, The Scarred Baron, will start.

how to Beat X'Fal, The Scarred Baron

X'Fal has a big mace that he swings around quickly, so now is a good time to get good at using the Evade button. Timing is important here, especially since Evade has a five-second cooldown, so you'll want to run away as soon as he raises the mace.

X'Fal can do more than just hit the mace up and down, which makes a damaging ripple on the ground. he can also sweep the mace across the ground. When you see him move the arm holding the mace back over the shoulder of the other arm, move under the other arm to avoid the swing. During this, he will also sometimes shoot flaming projectiles, so going around his back and around the other side of him is also helpful.

More importantly, X'Fal will form a pentagram on the ground at some point which will charge him up for a stronger attack. The red dots on his health bar show that he'll do this attack three times.

he will also send hellstormers to attack you during this time. But while you're killing them, you can also do more damage by hitting them while they're in the air. After he gets this power-up, he will jump into the air and try to land on you. You can quickly get out of the way because a circle will appear on the floor where he plans to land.

When you beat him, he drops a lot of things. Pick those up, and then use the rope at the back to go back to the Icehowl Taiga.

A hero's Return

Go back to the town of Nevesk to tell the people there that the demon has been defeated. Talk to Vani in the tavern, and she'll tell you how thankful she is. They don't have any money to give, but they have stew and drinks, which is good enough.

But these villagers aren't what they seem to be...

A hero's Reward

You'll be saved by Iosef before you're killed, but now you'll have to fight your way out.

Clear a path through the town and talk to Iosef when everyone is down. Then, talk to Vani's dead body in order to get the Chapel Key.

Prayers for Salvation

If you talk to him, you'll find out that he was the man who was talking about demons in the ruins earlier. he will tell you that the villagers gave him drugs, just like they gave you drugs, and that you need to go to the Chapel to find out more. Now that you have the Key, go to the Chapel. On the map, it is just south of you.

Go through the doors when you get there. You can pick up Blood Petals from the floor and use them. When you do this, a cutscene will start showing a Priest ringing the Chapel's bell back when the town was a bit busier.

But before he can finish talking to the villagers, petals will start falling from the ceiling. Then lilith will show up in a big way, and the truth about what happened to the villagers will come out.

Talk to Iosef again when the cutscene is over. If you ask him what he was doing in Nevesk, he'll say he was looking for the Town Priest, and we now know what happened to him. You can then ask how you got out of the Chapel. he'll tell you that you passed out and he pulled you out of the Chapel and set it on fire.

You'll tell him what you saw, and he'll tell you that he needs to take this information back to the Cathedral. he will then tell you to go north to meet a hermit who may have something to do with what is going on.

In Search of Answers

Follow the path on the map in the top right corner of the screen to find the hermit. When you leave the town's gate, you can also interact with an Altar of lilith.

Along the way, you'll face many different enemies, such as Skeletons, Wargs, hatchlings, Spiders, and Spider hosts. On the other side of that cave is the area where you can look for the hermit's cabin.

When you come out of the cave, go north to the Eastern Pass. Follow the path around until you reach an area with more space to explore. You can also find items here for harvesting. And the Windswept Cabin is over on the left.

Use the door to the cabin and go inside. The first thing you'll notice is the bookshelf, which you can interact with. You can also get information about the house from the Kettle by the fire, the Mortar and Pestle by the door, and the Jars on the wall.

Go to the bookshelf and do something to it to open a secret room. here, you can interact with Scattered Books on the floor that have Specimen Notes. There is also a Rusted Trap on the floor, but the Strange Skull in the back is more important.

If you talk to it, a cutscene will start with the hermit going home. This hermit's real name is lorath Nahr, and he can tell you a lot about what the villagers did to you and how lilith's plans for everyone are much bigger than we think. Next, you and your friend will go to Kyovashad.

Rite of Passage

Use the map in the top right corner to find the path north to Kyovashad. You'll meet a lot of enemies along the way, such as Fallen, a Fallen Shaman, and a Fallen Overseer. When you get to the city, a Guard will be standing in the street and tell you to stop before going in. Talk to lorath at this point.

he will tell you that you have to do a ritual to clean yourself before you can go into Kyovashad. he gets to skip, so you will have to do it by yourself. First, you'll need to go to the shrine and get a holy Cedar Tablet and write on it the sin that bothers you the most. You can be afraid, angry, proud, greedy, or feel nothing at all.

Then, throw it in the Brazier right next to it. After that, go back to the Guard and tell him it's done. You can now go and see lorath again.

Missing Pieces

Once you find lorath, he'll tell you that he needs to go to the Dry Steppes to find the Pale Man from your vision, but he needs you to get something for him from a Merchant in town. Before you do this, you can talk to him again and ask him more questions about Nevesk, Inarius, and lilith.

Now, go to town and find the Merchant. Tell him that lorath sent you, and he'll tell you that you have to pay for the weapon. You can get his Polearm for only 20 Gold, so go get it. he will also give you a Strange Amulet to give to lorath, so make sure to take that with you before you leave.

Give them both to lorath, and he'll tell you that the amulet is the mark of the horadrim, an ancient group of Scholars and Mages who swore to protect Sanctuary from demons. Even though there aren't many left, he tells you about someone who might help you on your journey.

The Prologue of Diablo 4 is now over.

ACT 1: A COLD AND IRON FAITH

Ill Tidings

After talking to lorath, you should head to the Cathedral of light. he thinks they could be very helpful in your fight against lilith, so go to the Cathedral in the northern part of Kyovashad.

Once you're inside, you need to talk to Reverend Mother Prava, who will be talking to Iosef. After they're done, she'll say that she's heard that a demon matching lilith's description was seen in Gale Valley. She tells you to check it out in Yelesna, so take the Knight's Report from her and leave the Cathedral.

You can also talk to Reverend Mother Prava and ask her how she knows lorath, what she knows about lilith, and what happened in Yelesna. This quest will be done when you pick up the report.

Tarnished luster

The next step is to go to Yelesna. So, go out of Kyovashad and away from the Cathedral by following the waypoint in the upper map. It can be found southeast of Kyovashad.

When you get to Yelesna, go to the building on the left and talk to Captain Ankers. Tell him you're looking for Vigo, and he'll tell you he's at the mining camp north of here, so you should head north. With this, the quest will be over.

The Knight and the Magpie

The next place you'll go is the mining camp at Pine hill. head out of the gates you came through to leave Yelesna and follow your map north of the town.

Talk to Vigo when you get to the mine. A girl named Neyrelle will show up and say that she saw lilith go into the mine and that she is with her mother right now. She'll ask for your help, and when the cutscene is over, you'll need to go back to Vigo to keep talking.

Once you tell him Prava sent you, he will let you into the mine. Neyrelle can take you with him to the Ore hoist, but it will be stuck, so you'll have to walk. Soon, Risen Miners will also come after you, so be ready to fight!

If you follow the path to the objective point, you will end up at the Condemned Mines, and if you go through them, this quest will be done.

Undertaking

Now is the time to go deeper into the mine and find lilith. Follow the path down and around, fighting enemies like skeletons and giant bats along the way. You'll soon come to some steps that go down. Follow the tunnel from here into a bigger room.

The lift won't work for Vigo, so he or she will have to find another way down. If you try to open the nearby door, you'll find that it's locked. however, Neyrelle will offer to fit through a nearby hole to open the door for you. As she does this, though, enemies will rush into the room and you'll have to fight them off.

After she opens it and kills all the enemies, go through the door and keep going through the tunnels.

You will end up in the Collapsing Depths if you do this. Through the door at the bottom of the stairs, go up to keep following the path across the bridge. You'll reach an Opening soon. You can go through it by interacting with it, which will end the quest.

Below

Talk to Vigo when you get to the other side. he'll tell them that the tunnels are closed and they're stuck without the Ore hoist, but Neyrelle will say she sees lilith and run away! Just follow her and then talk to her.

She will show you the statue and say that's the person she saw. Now you need to find a way down into the caves, so turn around and go back to where you came from. here is a place where you can climb down a cliff.

Follow the path down and around to get to the broken hoist. There's a Slain Demon stuck in it, which is bad. By doing something with it, you can get rid of it and fix the hoist, which will end this quest.

In her Wake

Talk to Vigo once the hoist has been fixed. he'll say that we need more help, but a noise from outside the nearby gate will cut him off. Go with Neyrelle to the huge Gate of Kasama to see what's going on.

As soon as it opens, go inside and you'll find the knights who have gone missing. One is also still moving, so go talk to him.

If you ask him who did it, he'll say it was one of the women Vigo sent with them, but she wasn't human... It turned out to be lilith. She led Neyrelle's mother Vhenard deeper into the cave, but he thinks nothing can stop her and that we should go back to Kor Valar and Prava for help.

Vigo agrees with the man and will decide to go back to Prava and the Cathedral, but Neyrelle wants to go deeper into the cave to find her mother. If you want to keep traveling with Neyrelle after Vigo leaves, you'll have to jump over the gap.

Follow the path until you get to a group of lilith's Blood Petals that are arranged in the shape of a symbol. When you talk to them, you'll be able to see a vision of lilith with Neyrelle's mother.

When it's done, go up the next set of steps and through the Ancient Gate. On the other side, a lot of Vile Ones will be waiting for you, so be ready to fight. Once you've taken care of them, you can also look at the Chalk Writing on the wall near the door to learn more about lilith.

Now, go down the steps and into Kasama more. The path to the right leads nowhere, so go left. here, you'll meet more enemies. After the fight, look near the broken back wall for more Chalk Writing that's worth looking into.

Keep going left until you reach another fork in the road. Right is another dead end, so go left and up the stairs to fight more enemies. You can also read some more Chalk Writing in here.

From here, go down the stairs to fight more enemies, then back up the stairs to fight more. When more enemies show up to fight, go under the archway near where you came up the stairs. In the next area, there is a small red picture on the ground from which you can see the area down below. Use it to find out what's going on.

This will show you where to go next, which is the Black lake. Go back to the room you were in before and down the other set of stairs. You should see footprints leading to the edge where you can climb down.

If you go up this next small set of stairs, you'll find the Gate of the Cradle, which is another big gate. You can read more Chalk Writing next to it before going inside. They will tell you about Rathma, who was the first person to master Necromancy as a power. he was the son of lilith and Inarius.

Head through the gate, and this quest will be done.

Storming the Gates

You can get into the Cradle from the inside. You'll go to the Courts of Dawn from here. When you get there, go up the stairs until you see another red lilith's Blood Petals symbol on the ground. Use it to see another vision of lilith and Vhenard together.

During this vision, you'll find out that they went looking for Rathma, lilith's son. Now, go ahead and open the Ancient Gate. Several different enemies will be waiting for you on the other side, so keep an eye out.

Once they're all down, you can go to the right or the left on the path, and they'll both meet up where you need to go. Also, watch out for traps on the floor as you run around. As shown below, they can look like little compasses on the ground or even like barrels that are about to explode.

Follow this path until you come to another large door. When you open it, Rohaksa, Gift of the Mother, will greet you. Once she's down, you can use lilith's Blood Petals on the ground to see another vision.

As soon as it's over, you can go through the Ancient Gate. Soon, you'll be in the Cloisters of Dusk.

At the bottom, you'll meet a lot of different enemies. When they are gone, go down the stairs on the right.

In the next area, you'll have to fight another group of enemies. After you've dealt with them, head out of this area on the other open path.

Take a right down this path to fight off more of these enemies, and then go up the stairs.

Now, go forward by taking the left path. In the next room, there will be more enemies. Take them down, and then go back to the left. If you go up this next set of stairs, you'll reach another Ancient Gate you can go through.

like other places, this room has an Ancient Gate, but this one has a wall around it. You won't be able to interact with any lilith's Blood Petals on the floor, so talk to Neyrelle for now. She will tell you that she thinks she can get rid of it, but you need to keep demons away from her while she does it.

Once the door is open, you can go through. When you come down the stairs, you'll reach the Mourning Shore. Going through it will finish this quest.

The Cost of Knowledge

Once you get through, you can go down this first set of stairs and find another stone with Vhenard's Records written on it, which doesn't sound good. Then go down the next flight of stairs.

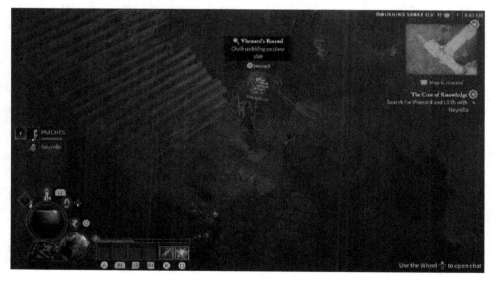

Stop at the healing Well to heal up before going to the next area. Then, go back up the stairs to find the Priest mentioned in Vhenard's Records and Vhenard standing in the middle of the floor.

Talk to Neyrelle right here, and she'll go talk to her mom. The conversation won't go well, so you'll have to fight Vhenard as a boss. You can read about her boss fight and how to beat her down below.

❖ how to Beat Vhenard

Vhenard is a hard boss to beat because she makes you move around and wait a lot. To defeat her, you need to focus on the demon servants she calls hell Spawn and kill them while she shoots projectiles at you from behind a barrier.

Vhenard's health bar has three dots, just like X'Fal, The Scarred Baron's. By the first marker, she will call up two hell Spawn to protect her. If you have a ranged weapon, it's easy to move around and shoot at them from a distance, but if you're a melee build, you'll have to dodge when they shoot their own projectiles. Go in, hit them a few times, and then roll around their sides, making sure to avoid Vhenard's fiery lines.

At mark two, things will really start to pick up. She will not only call up three hell Spawn, but she will also send hellstormers at you. First, run to the lower corner as soon as you see the red glowing pentagrams on the floor. This will give you a head start on the hell Spawn that appears here. Then, when the hellstormers come running toward you, quickly kill them. Once they're dead go back to the hell Spawn you started with.

Don't take them all down at once; take them down one at a time. But if you take too long, Vhenard will send out more hellstormers. So when you see more red pentagrams on the floor, you'll know they're coming.

Vhenard will have one last chaotic surprise for them once they're down. This is by far the hardest part, and you'll need a lot of patience. Now, five hell Spawn, a Pit lord, and hellstormers will be called forth. But that's not all. Once you get going, she'll call even more demons.

Start from the bottom corner, like you did before, to get a head start on killing the hell Spawn that appears here. They're your main targets, so you'll need to move around the room until they're alone so you can hit them. Slowly getting rid of the other demons also helps a lot.

After you beat her, she will drop different rewards for you to pick up. Also, this will finish the quest.

light's Guidance

After talking with Neyrelle, you'll need to go back to Kyovashad's Cathedral of light to talk with Prava. When you get there, Iosef will be there to meet you. Talk to him and tell him you need a holy blessing to keep looking for lilith.

he will tell you that Prava is at Kor Valar and that you need to go there. You can see from your map that you need to go northeast to get there, so leave town and start your trip. With this, the quest will be over.

Kor Valar

As soon as you walk into Kor Valar, you'll see Vigo sitting by a fire. If you talk to him, he'll tell you that he told Prava the truth about Vhenard, and he'll also come with you to talk to her.

Go inside the building she's in when you find it. You'll find her near a War Table that you can interact with to see that it's a map of Estuar with arrows pointing toward the city of Caldeum. Then you can talk to her and ask for the divine blessing.

She says you need to be made worthy first, so you'll have to go on a pilgrimage to the Shrine of the Penitent. When you finish this conversation, the quest will be done, and you'll have to get ready for another trip.

Pilgrimage

Get out of this building and go back all the way to the edge of town. To get to the Shrine, head southwest from the town.

When you get there, talk to Vigo to find out what you need to do. Then, start your short trip to the Shrine.

listen to the To the Sinner tablet when you get to the Altar of Purity, then pick up the Idol of the Faithful.

If you die while carrying this Idol, it will be left where you died, so you don't have to run back to the Altar to get it again.

To get this Idol to the next Altar, you'll have to fight through waves of enemies while carrying it. Before you can put it on the Altar of Martyrdom, you'll also have to fight a Vile Blight Bringer.

After killing the Vile Blight Bringer, listen to the To the Sufferer tablet next to the altar, and then take the Idol again.

Bring this Idol to the Altar of Redemption, just like you did before. This time your main boss will be a Blazing horror near the Altar. There will also be a number of Shambling horrors. Also, watch out for the pentagrams they make on the ground, because they will blow up!

Place the Idol on the Altar and listen to the To the Searcher tablet next to it. Then pick up the Idol again.

This time, the Idol needs to be taken to the Altar during the Anointed Ascent here, you'll have to fight a Fleshless Abomination and its followers before you can place the Idol. Once you've done that, you can listen to the To the Penitent tablet.

Now, you have to take the Idol to the Shrine of the Penitent. Talk to Vigo after you've put it down. he'll pray for a while, then turn around to talk to you and tell you that you're about to meet Father Inarius now that the pilgrimage is over. With this, the quest will be over.

Wayward

Now it's time to go to the Mistral Woods and meet up with Neyrelle. If you've already unlocked this travel point, you can find it close to Yelesna.

Once you get to the Woods, you'll have a large area to look through. She has gone to the north end of the circle, where the horadric Vault is. If you find a tree with glowing spots on it, you're getting close. When you get close, the way to the Darkened holt will open, and the quest will be done.

Shroud of the horadrim

Now is the time to go into the Darkened holt and find out where Neyrelle has gone.

You can get to the Winding Way by going through. Keep an eye out for Wood Wraiths and Phantoms as you go up and to the right on the snowy road.

Many parts of this area wind and loop around each other, so it's worth it to look around and see if there are any hidden treasures. At some point, you'll slide down into a place with more Wood Wraiths and Phantoms for you to fight. This is right here, and it will help you get around the rest of the area:

From here, go up the path and turn left at the first fork. Follow this path all the way to the end and go back up (see the maps above and below for help).

From the point shown on the map above, keep going to the right on the path and then turn south. Kill the enemies you encounter along the way, and when you reach a Sliding point, go down.

From here, go right until you reach a glowing portal where a Wolf will start talking to you. It will tell you to go through the portal, so do what it says.

This will lead you to the Vision of Tristram, which the Wolf says is a safe place where no one will hurt you. Go in with him and talk to him.

He will tell you that he was the one who rescued you in the mountains at the start. he wants to help you because he also wants to stop lilith, but he doesn't think the horadrim are the way to do it. Follow him to the living Gate and open it to learn more.

he will then show you how to get to another portal. If you talk to him again, he'll tell you that the horadrim will make a mistake one day, and he doesn't want you to be there when that happens. Then go through the portal and look for Neyrelle.

The portal will take you back to the Darkened holt, but this time the path will be a little different. Just ahead on the path, Neyrelle will be waiting for you.

She will have gotten lost trying to find the horadric Vault and needs your help to find it. Follow the path around to the left, and you'll end up in the Shadowed Glade, where some Phantoms, a hellcaller Wraith, and a Mirroring Wraith will be waiting for you.

Once you've beaten them, go to the back and interact with the Three-Faced Statue. With this, the quest will be over.

Fledgling Scholar

You'll go back to the Mistral Woods, and now that Neyrelle is with you, you can go to the horadric Vault. To do this, go back to the path that led you to the Darkened holt before. It is now clear.

If you follow it to the left, you'll get to the Vault quickly. Do something with it to go inside.

Talk to Neyrelle when you're done. She'll say that this is the place, but not what she was expecting. Follow her deeper into the Vault. To get here, all you need is one spell to cross the Black lake.

A spell will block the Study Door, so you'll have to figure out how to get through. Go straight to the nearby door and enter it. This will lead you to a Foyer with a room in the back. This room is full of Quillrats, so be ready to fight. The book you need to open the gate is also in this room. lesser Verses and Incantations is the name of the book. Bring it back to Neyrelle, and she'll open the gate for you.

Follow her inside and out the back door. This will take you further into the Vault, where you'll find another door that can only be opened with a spell. Talk to Neyrelle and ask her if she can use the spell to open the door for you. She will, but she will wait for you outside. You will have to go inside by yourself.

Once you get into the Study, be ready to fight many different demons as you look around. Go all the way to the back, where there is a large doorway with a healing Well in front of it. Only one thing can come from that. Fill up your supplies at the healing Well and head inside.

The book you need is being kept safe by Tchort, herald of lilith, a demon. She's not as hard as some bosses have been, but you still need to be patient with her. here is a list of what you need to do to beat her.

❖ how to Defeat Tchort, herald of lilith

You have to go through Tchort to get the Death harnessed: Theories of Rathma book for Neyrelle. She looks like other lilith followers you've seen, but unlike Vhenard, you'll only have to fight her. You can use both ranged and close-combat weapons to win this fight. Just be ready to spend a lot of time dodging her attacks.

Also, Tchort's health bar has three marks, and she has a lot of attacks to watch out for. In the first part of the fight, she swipes at you when she gets close, which you can avoid, and when you move away, she shoots three projectiles. You can also avoid them because they move in a straight line and don't try to get closer to you.

With these attacks, the best thing you can do is press the "Elude" button. She will also lunge right through you to knock you off balance and then shoot five projectiles at you in a straight line.

When these red orbs show up, move to the side to avoid them. You can easily get out of their way because they only move in a straight line. If she pushes you into the spinning cyclone around the book, it will slow you down and drain your health, so try to stay out of it as much as possible.

She can also make a pentagram on the floor below her to power up a Fire Orb that will grow and explode (the ripples on the floor show how big it is). You can hit the Fire Orbs to stop them from going off before they do.

When her health bar gets to the second mark, she'll keep using these attacks. After that, she'll start expanding the cyclone's range from around the book (you can see where it'll go by looking at the lines of the circle on the ground). It will pull you in if you get stuck in it. During this time, she'll also make several Fire Orbs to try to slow you down and get you caught in the cyclone's area of effect. You'll need to focus on getting rid of those first, before they go off.

By the third mark, she will have made almost 10 Fire Orbs, so take care of the ones closest to you so you don't get caught in an explosion. her attacks will stay the same from now on, so be careful and watch out for the Fire Orbs while you shoot from a distance or get close and dodge around her.

Once you've defeated her, take the book Death harnessed: Theories of Rathma, leave the boss room, and use the portal outside to go back to the Foyer and Neyrelle so you can give her the book.

It turns out that the book is a record of the spells and ideas that the first Necromancer, Rathma, came up with. This won't help Neyrelle cross the Black lake, but she thinks she can use this book to bring her mother back, who knows the ritual to cross, and have her help instead. This will finish the quest, so you should go back to the Black lake.

Crossing Over

Go back to the Mistral Woods and head to the mining camp at Pine hill that you visited with Neyrelle and Vigo earlier. It's just northeast of Yelesna. Once you're there, take the Ore hoist down.

Talk to Neyrelle again at the bottom to check on the plan. She says she'll tell you more on the way, so get going toward the Black lake. Talk to Neyrelle again when you get to the platform where you fought Vhenard before. This will start the ritual.

It will work out well! Vhenard will show you the way to the bridge so you can get to lilith. But you should talk to Neyrelle before you go across it.

She will stay and take care of her mother instead of going with you, so you'll have to do the next part by yourself. The quest will be done once the conversation is over.

Descent

Now is the time to cross the bridge. With this, you can get to the Necropolis of the Firstborn.

If you keep going down the path from there, you'll eventually see a vision of Rathma. he will say a few words and then disappear. You can keep going down the path.

You'll fight some Ghouls and a Shattering Revenant, and then you'll keep going down the path.

As you go on, you'll see a vision of Rathma again. he'll talk to you about prophecy, and then the vision will go away. When he's gone, keep going down the path.

You can get to the Central Chamber by going down the steps. Your path will be blocked, and you'll have to kill a Tumor of hatred to get through. There is one to the left of the door that you can get to by jumping. It will let you get through the archway in front of you. You'll have to kill four more tumors after this one.

Once you've done that, jump back over, go through the open area, and turn right to climb down from the bottom of these steps to reach the next tumor.

Just past the left staircase, if you keep going straight ahead on the path, you'll find another one.

After you get rid of it, go back and climb the wall to your right. Turn here to keep going down the path, and you'll have to fight through Fangstorms, a few Ghouls, and Shambling Corpses. At the end of this path, you'll also see another vision of Rathma, which shows you're on the right track.

Take a left and go up the stairs to get into a bigger area. Keep going left on the path, which will take you to another tumor. Get rid of it, and then go behind it and climb down the wall.

Follow the path to the left until you reach a set of stairs on the right, across from where you came up. Then go up. On the other side, go left toward the next set of stairs, but turn left at the next set of stairs. here, duck under the branch and then cut off the growth.

Now, take this path back to the stairs and go up. When you get to the top of the second flight of stairs, you'll be on a landing. To keep following the path, go left around the broken stairs.

The vision of Rathma will come back and then go away. Once he's gone, just keep going down the path and you'll soon get to the last tumor. Move ahead of it to climb down the wall after you've cleared it.

When you get to the bottom, you'll see a vision of Inarius and Rathma talking to each other. After you've heard what they have to say, kill the last tumor that has appeared to get to the Central Chamber.

You'll see another vision of Inarius and Rathma talking while you're on this path. listen in, then keep moving. Not long after that, you'll also reach a lookout where you can see the Balance's Sanctum. It's marked by a red symbol on the floor. After that, keep going down the path.

You'll soon reach a healing Well where you can refill your health items. Do this before going further.

In this next area, lilith's lament will be the boss you have to fight. here is a breakdown of how to approach this fight and how to beat him.

❖ *lilith's lament: how to Beat It*

During this fight, you'll only have to worry about lilith's lament, but he has a lot of other moves to worry about.

In the beginning, lilith's lament will fire one purple projectile at a time and then drop puddles of brown sludge on the ground. If you land in one of these puddles, you'll slow down and lose health, so it's best to move quickly around this arena. But a brown circle on the floor will show you where a puddle will land.

If you use a long-range weapon, you should keep moving and only stop to fire a few shots at a time. For melee builds, you should rush at him and hit him a few times before moving away. You have to weave in and out because he can also drop sharp spikes around him that can hit you.

When you hit the second mark on his health bar, a Knight Penitent will come to help. This helper will be very useful, especially with the next attack from lilith's lament. You should listen when the Knight tells you to stay close Blood will be on the floor, so go to the Knight Penitent and hide under his barrier. During this time, lilith's lament can't be attacked by anything either.

Once the blood has stopped flowing, you can go back outside. Unfortunately lilith's lament will have more attacks than just that one. Now, his hand can change into a whip. luckily, a red slice on the ground will show you where the whip will be going so you can move out of the way.

At this point, he'll bring out rolling brown sludge, which you'll have to move around, along with the still-falling puddles. Brown rectangles on the sides of the arena show where these come from. Where they gather is where they'll start rolling across the arena, so you can figure out the best way to get to where you want to go before they leave. They also don't leave a long brown trail behind them, so you can move behind them when you don't see brown on the floor.

All of these attacks will show up along with his usual ones, so you'll have to move slowly to get your attacks in. The Knight Penitent will be able to help get rid of him, and the glowing light that ripples through the ground is also coming from him, so don't be afraid.

At the next marker, he'll cover the ground in blood again, so go to the Knight Penitent for safety. After that, go back out and keep fighting. In addition to his usual attacks, he will also gather 10 purple projectiles around him and fire them at you. With this, try to move in a circle around the arena to avoid them. They don't remember where they came from, so it's easy to get away from them.

As the fight goes on, the brown sludge and drops will start to take up more space on the floor as they fall and roll more often. You'll need to keep moving around and sneaking up on him when you can.

After the third red marker and again when he has a tiny bit of health left, he'll cover the floor in blood again, so hide under the Knight Penitent's shield.

After you beat him, he will drop a number of rewards for you to pick up. Then, talk to the Knight Penitent who came to the rescue.

Wasn't it Vigo? he doesn't make it, but he does drop Vigo's Protecting Amulet, which is a legendary Amulet.

After you pick it up, go forward along the path to go after lilith. Along the way, you'll see another vision of Rathma and Inarius talking to each other. After you've listened, keep going. Inside the next room, you'll find a dead body and a symbol made of lilith's Blood Petals on the floor. When you talk to the Petals, a cutscene about what happened here with lilith will start.

When the cutscene is over, the quest will be done.

ACT 2: THE KNIFE TWISTS AGAIN

An Unforeseen Visit

When you get to Eldhaime Keep, you'll need to talk to the watch commander Commander Antje, as she is called, is on the left side of the Keep. She will tell you where Donan is and that you should first talk to the guard at the door. The entrance is at the point shown below.

Talk to the guard, and he'll tell you that Donan is upstairs with his son in the Great hall, so go there to find him.

You'll hear them talking on the second level up from where you are, so take the stairs on the left to get there. Once they're done talking, talk to Donan and tell him what lorath said. The quest will be done once the conversation is over.

Dark Omens

When you get there, you'll need to talk to Steward Wilfred, who is right at the Manor's entrance.

he will tell you about something scary that happened in Donan's Study, so go there and go downstairs to see what happened.

When you get down there, talk to the Blood Petals on the floor to start a cutscene that tells you what happened.

You'll hear a signal horn in the distance when it's done... Outside, something is going on. Get back to the top floor and get ready to fight through waves of enemies.

Talk to Donan when they're all down. The quest will be done once the conversation is over.

Encroaching Shadows

You can find Braestaig just north of where you are, at the place marked on the map below.

When you get to the area, first interact with the Waypoint to make fast travel possible. Then, look around in different places to see if you can find any signs of lilith. Chieftain Asgail will eventually talk to you about protecting the town from ghosts. Talk to her when she's done.

Yorin, a young man, will offer to go with you to Airidah's house. Talk to him when you're ready to start the quest. he will tell you that the roads are foggy and that the fastest way to get there is to go east through the Weeping Cairns

When you open your map, you'll see a yellow circle to the east. This is the area you need to look in to find the entrance to the Weeping Cairns. Start your journey with Yorin when you're ready. he will just keep going after you.

You can get to it from a climbing point near the northern end of the circle:

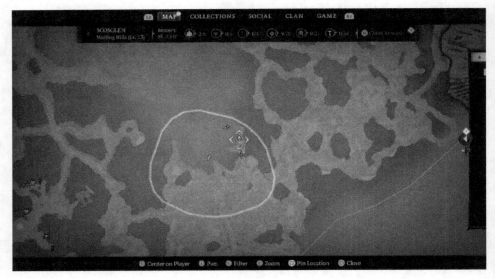

Yorin will tell you that the passage is blocked when you get to the front door. If you talk to him, he'll tell you that it needs a chant to open, but enemies are coming, so you'll have to protect him while he does the chant.

Once all of the enemies are dead, he will have opened the door successfully, and you can go inside. If you go to the Weeping Cairns, the quest will be done.

Exhuming the Forgotten

Once you and Yorin are inside the Weeping Cairns, you'll have to go deeper into the dungeon until you reach a locked door. When you're ready, talk to Yorin.

he'll tell you that the door is locked with an earthen seal, and that to open it, you'll need to put a Wardstone in the Runic Standing Stone to the left of the door. You can find it in the nearby Cairns. To start exploring, go to the area to the left of the door and interact with the Chamber Door.

You will run into Spirit enemies right away, so be ready to fight them all as you move through the Cairns.

You'll eventually find an Overgrown Wardstone Altar. Destroy it along with the enemies around it, grab the Wardstone, and head back to Yorin.

Put the Wardstone in the Runic Standing Stone to the left of the door, and Yorin will start speaking Druidic to open it. You can go through when the door opens.

Follow the path up and around to find another Chamber Door. Interact with it to open it and head through. here, you'll find an Altar that has writing on it If you talk to Yorin again, he will start to read it.

he says that the words are actually an elegy written by Airidah, and that this Altar is a memorial to those who died fighting Astaroth. Not long after that, though, the ghosts from the memorial will start talking, and they don't sound too happy.

Then, angry Wildwoods will start attacking you from the ground up. Take them down, and then keep moving through the Weeping Cairns by going back the way you came.

You'll soon come to another Chamber Door. Open it and go through to find the Cairn of the Elders. It has demonic scars, is surrounded by blood, and has Druid ruins written on it that can bring the dead back to life. Someone we know has definitely been here.

Talk to Yorin here, and he'll tell you more about what he sees. Most of the work here looks like it was done by Airidah, and he will wonder why she has joined lilith's side. Even though it's a shame, she will need to be stopped. So, go to the other side of the room and look for the exit out of the Weeping Cairns. You can also listen to Writings of Airidah's Concern, which you can find near the door.

Climb up and out of the cave to get to Ancestor heights. With this, the quest will be done.

harrowed lament

When you open your map, you'll see that this whole area of Ancestor heights is circled. This means that you'll have to look for Airidah quite a bit.

As you go up the paths here, you'll come across Risen Remains that are bringing Spirits up from the ground. After you kill the Remains and all of the Spirits in the area, two people will run out of the house on the right. Yorin will know one of them and walk over to talk to him.

Talk to Arlo after they're done talking and ask him what happened. he'll say that Airidah came through here with "a horned woman" (we know who that is) and that the two of them went up the hill called Solitude. But there's too much fog to get to the hill, so you'll have to get rid of the Risen Remains to clear it away, since it seems to be coming from them.

You'll only have to get two, which are marked in different places on the map. Mark them on the map, and then start going in that direction.

At each location, you'll have more than one Spirit to help you fight the Risen Remains, so be ready. After they've been dealt with, go back to Yorin and Arlo.

Speak with Arlo again and tell him to head to Braestaig, which is a much safer spot for him and his daughter than here, given lilith's presence. Yorin will escort them safely back, and it's now time for you to track down Airidah and lilith. With this, the quest will be over.

Apex of Misery

On the map below, Airidah is just to the north of where you are on Solitude.

As you get closer to her, you will run into two Risen Remains that have risen from the ground. But these ones are helped by Spirits, so you have to take out their connection before you can take them down.

After getting rid of all of these enemies and the two Risen Remains, keep going up the path until you reach her. On the way up, though, you'll face a lot more enemies, so don't get too comfortable. Not to mention the voice of Airidah taunting you the whole time.

At some point, you'll find her sitting on top of the hill, playing music and enjoying the stormy sky. She will tell you that only one of you will win, which is true, because she will quickly get ready for a fight. here is a list of what you need to do to beat Airidah, Keeper of the Dead.

❖ how to Defeat Airidah, Keeper of the Dead

When you first see Airidah on top of Solitude, she is playing her instrument and looking very calm. But things change quickly when the battle starts and she asks you to prove yourself.

At first, Airidah's main attack will be to call down lightning. You can see where each bolt will hit, though, because there are blue circles on the ground Move around those to get to her.

She will also teleport around the room after a few hits, so be ready to do a lot of running to catch her and avoid the circles on the floor. During this time, she will also call up small tornadoes that can push you back, so be careful to avoid them as you circle around her.

She will teleport to the middle of the room after the first marker, where you can get some more healing potions. At this point, she will call upon two Spirits to help her fight and protect her. You'll have to kill them first before she can attack again, all while avoiding her lightning and tornado attacks that will come from all directions.

Now that they're dead, she'll do the same tricks she did in the first phase, so you can keep attacking and dodging as you did before.

She won't call on Spirits again until the last dot on her health bar is gone. like before, kill her minions first while dodging her attacks (there are more lightning bolts and tornados now), which will make her easier to kill. But this time, she will have four Spirits, so you'll have to move around a bit more than last time. Once the Spirits are gone, you can go back to your usual attacks to kill her.

Walk over to her and talk to her again once you've beaten her. She will give up and say that you are stronger. But when you ask her what she gave lilith, you'll find out something shocking... She will tell her that she told her how to get Astaroth out of jail. At least you now know where she's going next.

The quest will be done once this conversation is over.

Parting Embers

This main story quest just has you go back to Braestaig, so just go there. Talk to Yorin when you get there. he'll tell you that he has to go tell his father what happened and what lilith did.

The quest will be done once the conversation is over.

Feral Nature

To complete this quest, you'll need to go to Tirmair and talk to the knights there about lilith. On the map below, you can see where to find them.

When you get to Tirmair, the knights you need to talk to will be right next to the Waypoint, which you'll need to unlock. Talk to Knight-Captain Razia here and ask her if she's seen a demon pass through. She will say that she has... a woman with horns!

The last time she was seen, she was in the Moors, where only a man named Nafain lives now. To find him, you'll have to go to the Boglann Stone Circle. This place is in a yellow circle on your map, just northeast of where you are now.

To get to the inner circle area, where Nafain's house is, you'll have to climb up a small cliff. he's not there, and the stone next to it has a very unwelcoming message written on it.

When you're done reading it, Nafain's wolf will appear nearby. Once he's calmed down a bit, he'll help you find Nafain. A very good dog, indeed. The quest will be done after this conversation.

The Beast Within

Follow Nafain's wolf to his master's location, now that you have a helpful guide. The path to him is covered in blood and enemies, so it's not a good place at all.

After you fight your way through this bloody place, you'll find Nafain in the heart of the Moors in a terrible state. When you find him, talk to him. he'll tell you that lilith did this, but he'll also tell you where she went and help you find her. Follow his instructions and head north to find her and find out where his blood is gathering.

The quest will be done once this conversation is over.

The Path of Rage

Follow Nafain's wolf to his master's location, now that you have a helpful guide. The path to him is covered in blood and enemies, so it's not a good place at all.

After you fight your way through this bloody place, you'll find Nafain in the heart of the Moors in a terrible state. When you find him, talk to him. he'll tell you that lilith did this, but he'll also tell you where she went and help you find her. Follow his instructions and head north to find her and find out where his blood is gathering.

The quest will be done once this conversation is over.

Fangs of Corruption

Start walking down the path inside the Untamed Thicket, and you'll eventually find lilith's Mark on the ground. Interact with it to see a vision of her, then keep going. Just around the corner and up ahead on the left is another Mark. First, talk to it before moving on.

This vision is especially interesting because she will talk about a "amalgam of rage" being created in this place, which could be fueled by Nafain's blood. If you keep going down the path, you'll soon find another Mark from lilith that gives you more information about how dangerous this creature she made is.

At the end of this path, you'll come to a branch that you'll have to duck under to get to the Corrupted Spawning Ground, where Nafain's blood has been going. Now you can see what lilith meant when she talked about this mix of anger.

But for now, it's still in the womb. You'll have to fight several Werewolves and Wolves until the big beast is ready to make its grand entrance.

As it turns out, this beast is a big, tough creature that looks like Cerberus. Even though he only has a small amount of health, it will be hard to hurt him But don't worry, you're not meant to do that right now.

After a while, it will hear lilith's voice calling it, and it will run away. With this, the quest will be over.

Stemming the Flow

Now that the Spawn of hatred has left and is going back to lilith, you'll need to go back to Nafain and tell him what happened and why his blood was being used. Then, go back to the heart of the Moors.

When he talks to you, he will tell you that he did have something to do with this. he made a deal with lilith because he wanted to destroy the Knights Penitent. In exchange, he told her where Astaroth is hidden: in Eldhaime.

Now you know where to go next, but he will want you to stop the corruption before you leave. When you do that, the quest will be done.

Buried Secrets

You now know, thanks to what Nafain told you, that lilith is probably going to Eldhaime Keep to find Astaroth. So go back there.

Once you get there, you'll see that the place is full of enemies, which is a sure sign that lilith has been here. Fight your way to the main gate, but it will be blocked by debris, so you'll have to find a different way to get there.

Go to the other end of the Keep to find Commander Antje and a blockade you can break through. Ask her where Donan is by talking to her.

She'll say that he's probably still inside, but lilith got through and couldn't be stopped. Uh oh. We need to find Donan. If you finish this conversation, this quest will be done.

In Ruins

head left from where Commander Antje is to enter Eldhaime Keep through a large door. Once you get inside the Stormed Battlements, you can start making your way to the Great hall. Since this area is a dungeon, each player will get a different set of directions, but they will all end up in the same place.

At some point, you'll reach the glowing entrance to the Great hall. Use it to open the door and go inside to find Donan.

You can find him at the bottom of the stairs on the main level, where he is burying some of his dead soldiers. Talk to him after he finishes praying. he'll say that lilith and her new Spawn of hatred tore through the place and are now looking for Astaroth in an old room under the keep. You'll have to go down together to find her. The quest will be done when the cutscene is over.

Entombed legacy

Follow Donan up the steps to the Eldhaime Barracks when the conversation is over. You'll also have to look for Yorin along the way, since he hasn't been seen yet.

Move around the Barracks until you reach a doorway that looks like a yellow circle in the upper right corner of your map. You'll also see a few dead Knights who were supposed to protect Yorin, which is not a good sign.

If you go through this doorway, you'll find a ladder that leads to the Earthen Passage. Follow the path through here to get to the tomb of Astaroth.

Donan will run toward your goal as you get closer, so you'll need to follow him now. At some point, you'll get to the chamber with the soulstone, but Yorin won't be there. What lilith wanted happened, but where did Yorin go? You have to interact with lilith's Mark on the floor to find the answer, which is on the other side of the room.

After this cutscene, you'll be taken back to the Great hall and told to talk to Donan again to figure out what to do. he will tell you that he has studied the soulstone and knows it will take time for Astaroth to gain power over Yorin through it. Your next step will be to go to a place called Cerrigar, where Astaroth is likely to be.

The quest will be done once this conversation is over.

Shadow Over Cerrigar

After talking to Donan, you'll need to meet up with him in Cerrigar to find Astaroth and lilith. This area is just north of where you are now, at the point on your map shown below.

Donan is just outside lower Cerrigar once you get to the town. Both lilith and Astaroth are already here, and their arrival has caused a lot of chaos.

Follow Donan to the lower Cerrigar Gate, and a cutscene will start showing you the terrifying demon lilith has brought back to help her. After this scene is over, the quest will be done, and you'll fight Astaroth right away.

As the World Burns

Astaroth is a very scary boss right away, especially because he is so big. You can use this to your advantage by dodging under him and trying to get behind him to deal damage. Most of his attacks are also in front of him, like a swipe from his staff or the Spawn of hatred breathing fire. he will also howl to call Werewolves to help him and call down fireballs that you'll need to avoid.

As soon as the fight starts, several Werewolves will join him to fight. The Spawn of hatred, on the other hand, will shoot fire at you as soon as it appears, so you'll need to move around or under it to get behind it and start doing damage. You should only hit him a few times, though, because he will soon jump away in a different direction, and if you're not careful, his feet can crush you.

Astaroth will also swing his staff in front of him, which is another reason why you should stay behind him at this time. In general, the most dangerous place will be in front of him, so moving around him or to his sides will help a lot. You aren't completely safe back there, though, because he will eventually throw fireballs at you. Keep an eye out for red circles on the ground and stay out of them to get around these.

Each time he hits the first and second markers on his health bar, which give you healing potions, he will move to a new spot. You'll need to follow him as he moves to keep fighting, but even though he's moving, his attack patterns will stay the same (though they'll happen more often), so you can keep fighting him the same way you did before.

Once he's down, Donan will run over to try to free Yorin from Astaroth's control. It's too bad, but it won't work. Donan needs to be left alone to mourn for now, so go to the gate and talk to the guard. When you finish this conversation, this quest and Act 2 will be done.

ACT 3: THE MAKING OF MONSTERS

The Spreading Darkness

At the start of this Act, you'll have to go back to Ked Bardu and find lorath. As you can see on the map below, this is on the western side of Sanctuary.

When you get to Ked Bardu, lorath will be in a bad shape... Talk to Daruuk, the man next to him, and ask him what happened. he and his friend, Khelit, will say that he came to town a few days ago looking for the Pale Man, a servant of lilith, and wasn't too happy with what he found out about him.

Interact with lorath when the conversation is over to wake him up and ask him about the Pale Man. he will say that he used to work for horadrim and that his name was Elias when he did. he was the one who brought lilith to Sanctuary, which made lorath angry.

Your next big step is to find out where Elias is, but before you can do that, you need to find out more about what's been going on with him around here. Find a woman named Teckrin in town and ask her if she knows anything about the Orbei Monastery. You can find her just east of where you are now in town.

She will say that she hasn't heard from Orbei, but she has some other interesting news to share... It's been said that the Pale Man was recently seen in the Abahru Canyons, which Iorath is sure to be interested in hearing. Tell him about this new piece of information.

Since he wrote to Orbei the day he got here, he will be worried that they haven't replied, but he will also want to check out the Canyons. You can decide where you want to go next. The quest will be over after this talk.

If you want to see the Canyons first, go to our page for the Whittling Sanity quest. Or, if you want to see the Orbei Monastery, go to the Suffering Disquiet quest page. For that quest, though, you should be at least level 20.

Suffering Disquiet

As the map below shows, the Orbei Monastery is south of where you are.

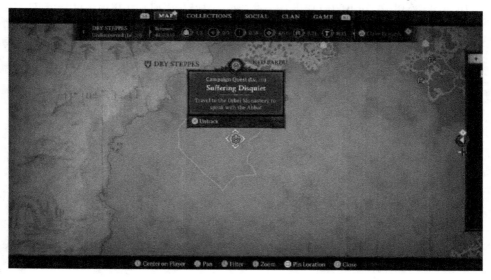

When you get there, go inside and start looking for the Abbot.

Someone or something has already been through the halls of the Monastery, because you'll find many Slain Monks as you move through them. But the first dead monk you see when you enter will also have a Message From the Abbot that you should listen to before you continue your journey.

As you move through the Outer Cloister, a small yellow circle will show up on your mini-map. This will lead you to a door that you can't open without a Crusader Skull. This thing isn't too far away, which is good.

It's in the hands of Sister Martina, who was attacked and is in a big room behind where you are right now. Pick up the Crusader Skull from her dead body and put it on the pedestal by the door.

This will unlock the door so you can go inside and keep looking. On your way through here, you'll also meet a lot of Phantoms, so be ready to fight.

At some point, you'll get to a room with a still-alive Monk in it. Talk to him and find out where the Abbot is. he will say that the Abbot let the Pale Man in and that the Pale Man took "forbidden knowledge."

Before he can tell you any more, you'll have to fight off Vengeful Phantoms. Once they are down, keep looking for the Abbot.

You'll find him hidden behind a big, locked door for the Archive that leads to a healing Well. When you talk to the door, you'll find out how to open it. The writing on it says that you need to find the three Secret litanies to get into the Inner Cloister, which is just past the door. The good news is that they will be marked on your map, and they are all very close to each other.

Once you know the Secret litanies, you can go back to the door to the Archive and interact with it to say them out loud. This will open the door, letting you go inside the Archive.

Inside, the Archive is on fire, and the Abbot is sitting in the middle of it all. If you talk to him, you'll find out that he let Elias in and that Elias took the information he needed to call a lesser Evil. Not only that, but he also killed every Scholar at the Monastery.

As the Abbot screams for forgiveness, all of the Vengeful Spirits will come out and form the Eidolon of Orbei. This boss's attack patterns and information on how to beat him are listed below.

❖ how to Defeat Eidolon of Orbei

When the boss fight starts, one of the first moves the Eidolon of Orbei will make looks almost like a small red vortex. You'll want to avoid or go around this, as it will not only drain your health but also make it hard to see.

he will also teleport around the room and call up Bone Walls to try to trap you in his red vortices. If you get stuck in a corner, the Bone Walls can be very annoying. To avoid this, be ready to switch between attacking him and attacking these Walls. he might even put up a Wall around himself that you have to break down to get to him.

As the fight goes on, he will keep attacking in the same way, but he will use vortices and bone walls more often, so watch out as you move around the room to get to him and lower his health.

Once he's down, you can get a number of things from him, but the Gospel of the Mother is the most important. If you do something with this, you'll learn important things about Elias and what his goal was here. This quest will also be done when this fight is over.

Whittling Sanity

lorath will be near a well when you get to Abahru Canyon. If you finished Suffering Disquiet before this, you can tell him what happened to the Abbot at the Orbei Monastery and what happened there. Mainly, it means that Elias now has the power to call a lesser Evil, but it's not clear which one.

he'll tell them that the lesser Evils are almost as powerful as the Primes, and that if he's able to call one, everyone could be in a lot of danger. Now that you know where he is, you can go look for him in Abahru Canyon. When you open your map, a small area east of where you are will be circled, as shown on the map below. Get yourself there.

When you get to the area in the circle, you'll find a hell Rift. lorath will say that he can shut it, so you should just focus on killing the enemies who are coming at you.

Once they're all dead, keep going north on the path until you get to a house. Inside, you'll have to search for information about Elias. On the candle-lit table at the entrance, you'll find a Demonic Scroll and a Page from Genbar's Journal. You can read the Broken Carvings in the next room. In the last room, you'll find a Dead Mercenary next to a Bloody Statue of lilith.

Once lorath gets to the statue, you can talk to him and tell him what you found, then listen to what he says. he'll tell us it's too late, but you can still find the man who used to live here, Genbar, and ask him about Elias. Find Genbar by going out the door to the left of the Bloody Statue. The map below shows that he is just to the northwest of where you are now.

When you get close to him, he will be on his knees praying. When he is done, you can talk to him. lorath will ask him where "Master Elias" is, but he won't like that question and will call you both liars, which will start a boss battle. here is a list of what you need to do to beat Genbar, the Shrine-Keeper.

❖ how to Defeat Genbar, the Shrine-Keeper

In the middle of this room, you'll see another hell Rift like the one you saw earlier. Genbar will use this to call more enemies to help him fight, but they usually die quickly, so you can focus on Genbar again. Some will run up to you and attack, but others, like the Succubus, will shoot purple projectiles that you'll need to watch out for and avoid.

Genbar will also make red pentagrams on the floor. If you get stuck in them (shown by a small skull above your head), you'll be confused, so try to move around them as you attack him.

he will ask Elias for help halfway through the fight, saying that his enemies are here... and he will answer. he will tell lorath that he has a "gift" for her—a demon named Mahmon. Now you'll have to fight both Genbar and the demon. Genbar's attacks will stay the same, which is good news, but Mahmon will have a few more tricks up its sleeve.

If you get too close, Mahmon will attack you with its sword and also build rock walls to trap you. When these come out, you should try to kill them first before moving on with the fight. The best way to beat him is to move around behind him or shoot him with a ranged weapon. Once he's down, Genbar's usual attacks with his hired enemies will be all you have to worry about.

Once Genbar is down, talk to lorath at the foot of the Shrine where Genbar was praying earlier. he'll say that Elias seems ready to do something big now that he has "all he needs," and that you and Genbar need to figure out what it is. You're lucky to have a helpful, now-dead demon nearby. Since it probably lived on sacrifices, it might know something.

lorath will want to take it back to Ked Bardu to have it looked at, so meet him there. With this, the quest will be over.

A Moment to Collect

Now that the demon is back at Ked Bardu, you'll need to meet up with lorath there to find out what's inside it and, hopefully, find a clue that will lead you to Elias.

When you get back to Ked Bardu, lorath will be at the city's southern edge. If you talk to him, you can follow him into the building next to him to look into the demon. Inside, you'll find a medallion that belonged to the ruler of the royal house of Guulrahn, so that's a good place to go next to find Elias.

When this scene is over, the quest will be done.

Brought low

Now that you've found the medallion in the demon's stomach, you know where to go to find Elias: a city called Guulrahn. Open your map to start figuring out how to get there. As the map below shows, it is southeast of where you are now.

lorath will be at the hidden Overlook when you get to Guulrahn. Talk to him to find out what you should do next. he'll say it's too hard to get through, but a young woman standing next to him will say she knows someone who can.

This woman is Zolaya, who lorath already knows. She will tell lorath that someone named Oyuun is stuck inside Guulrahn and that she may be the only one who can help them find the tunnel to get inside the palace. lorath won't want to go inside to look for her, so you'll offer to go down instead.

She will tell you that if you want to know where to look, you should find the Market Square because that's where Oyuun's house is, so that's your next goal. When the cutscene is over, climb down the cliff where lorath was standing to get into Guulrahn. Also, this will finish the quest.

The City of Blood and Dust

When you get to Guulrahn, you will land on a roof in the Sanguine Alley. You can get to the streets by dropping down from this roof.

Follow the path around to start your journey through the city, and be ready to face many different kinds of enemies, but especially cannibals.

At some point, you'll see a small yellow dot on your mini-map. This means you're getting close to the Market Square. When you get there, go up the first ladder you see on your right.

Follow the path straight ahead on this upper level, jump across to the other side, and then turn left. If you keep going down this path and jump over another gap, you'll end up near a young woman whose screams you can hear.

help her get rid of the enemies in her house, and then talk to her. When asked about Oyuun, she won't know her by name, but she will say that the cannibals have been rounding up a few people and bringing them to the prisons. This is the next place you should look for.

From where this woman is standing, go behind her and use the sliding point to get down to the lower level. From there, head north (away from where you came in) to start looking for the prison.

Follow the path straight ahead and around until you reach the Gate house. On the right, duck into a small stone room to find the Gate Control and a Gorger you need to kill. Talk to the Gate Control to open the prison gate, then go back out the way you came in to go inside.

Once you're inside, you can start moving through the Cells and killing cannibals as you go. At the back, an enemy named Akil, Jailer of the Weak, will drop down and fight you before you can move on. Take him out and take the Guulrahn Prison Key from his body. This will let you open the door to the next room where Oyuun is.

Talk to her when you see her. She will say that she knows a safer way out than going back the way she came, which means going to the old prison wing You'll need to go back into the room where you fought Akil and follow Oyuun to the right to get there. Use the Key you found to open the cell door, and then in the next room, break the wall in front of you.

Once you get past this broken wall, you'll have to break down another wall to get into another cell block full of enemies. When they're down, go forward and to the right to get to another door that you can open.

Keep moving through these areas and killing enemies until you reach a crack in the wall that leads back outside to The Trail of Bones. When you get outside, your quest will be done.

Small Blessings

Talk to Oyuun now that you are outside of Guulrahn on The Trail of Bones. Ask her if she's ready to move on, and then lead her back up the path and around to Zolaya and lorath.

After they see each other again and Oyuun shows them how to get to the palace through the secret tunnel, talk to lorath. he'll say that he's surprised by your connection to lilith, since you haven't "gone dark" yet, and that maybe he's wrong about you. When you do this short thing, the quest will be done.

Whispers from the Past

You can find lorath in the nearby caverns, which are marked on the map below.

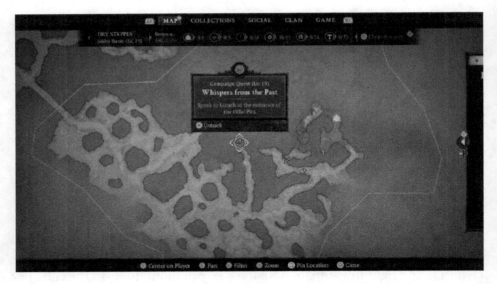

Talk to him when you get there. he'll tell you that he's been thinking about which of the lesser Evils Elias is trying to call up and that it could be either Duriel or Andariel. The first one thrives on physical pain, while the second one likes to cause mental and emotional pain. It's clear that both are very, very bad news. lorath is afraid that if either one is called, more cities will be destroyed like Guulrahn. hopefully, you can find Elias before it's too late.

Start your journey into the Offal Pits after the conversation. Inside, you'll have to go back and forth between the paths until you find a secret alcove. It's not too hard to find, though, because it looks like a big door to open.

When you talk to lorath, he will do what Oyuun tells him to do, which is to open the door and go inside. When you get to the top of the ladder and turn left, you'll see a big hole in the wall that leads into the palace. Stop here for a moment and talk to lorath to hear what's going on.

After this short cutscene, which shows that Elias wants to bring Andariel into the world, keep going around the path until you come to a door you can open to go inside the palace.

Once you're inside, go through The Bowels until you come to a big staircase that leads up to the Tyrant's Court. From here, go to the end on the right to find a second staircase that leads up to Elias' Throne Room. here, you'll face a boss called Mother's Judgement. You can see how to beat this boss and how she attacks in the next section.

❖ How to Beat Mother's Judgment

There are many different ways to get hurt by Mother's Judgment. The first thing you'll notice about her attack is a spell she casts with her hands. She'll also make big red sparking circles on the ground that will explode if you get caught in them.

During this time, she will teleport to the farthest circle away, so try to head in that direction to get to her faster and deal damage. Once they're gone, they'll also shoot some red projectiles that you'll have to avoid. As you can see, a lot is happening right from the beginning.

Along with these, she will make a row of smaller red circles that go off very quickly. These can be a few, a long line, or even three lines coming together, so it's best to move to the side where they are as soon as you see them. But luckily, these are all of her attack patterns, so once you've learned them, you're good to go for the rest of the fight!

And, in more good news, this boss can be stunned, even if it's just for a short time. But if it works, you should be ready to do as much damage as you can before she gets back up.

Move to the left side of the room after the fight to get to an area blocked by a red Ward of Sealing. Act on it to get rid of it, and then go inside.

This will lead you to Elias' Sanctum, where there are lots of interesting things to look at. On the left side of the room, near a large statue, you'll find a Torn-Out Page to read and an Old Worn Map of Mt. Civo. In the back right you'll find Elias' lockbox with some treasures inside, and on the right side of the room, you'll find Elias' Journal to read.

Once you've found everything important, talk to lorath to tell her what you've found. he'll tell you that you need to go to the Temple of Primes on Mt. Civo because that's where Andariel will be called. So, that's where you should go next. But you need to find a way out right now.

he'll say that it's probably behind the bookshelf, which he would have learned from lorath, and he's right! Follow the path to the hidden Overlook, then talk to lorath once more. he'll tell you to hurry up so you can catch up with Elias, so get ready for a trip. Also, this will finish the quest.

Through the Dark Glass

For this quest, you need to meet lorath at the base of Mt. Civo, which is shown on the map below.

When you get there, talk to lorath to find out what to do next. he will tell you that you can't just walk in, which is sad. To open the way, you need to find three shrines for Mephisto, Baal, and Diablo and ask for their blessings. It's dangerous, but you have to do it. Find the first one on your map to start. Just to the north of where you are will be Baal's shrine. Mark it on your map and go there first.

To start the blessing, you'll need to talk to the Altar of Destruction when you get there. Once it's done, you'll need to go to Diablo's shrine. To get there, keep going to the right until you reach a wall, and then climb up it to reach the Altar of Terror.

Repeat the same pattern as before by interacting with the Altar and accepting the blessing. Then, head south of here to Mephisto's shrine at the location below.

Talk to lorath first when you get there. he'll tell you that this blessing will be a little different because you have lilith's blood in you, and he's right. Start by interacting with the Altar of hatred. This time, a portal will open up next to you.

If you walk through it, you'll end up in front of Mephisto himself, who is in the form of a familiar wolf. he will tell you that he was with you in the cave and in the Shroud of the horadrim from the start!

he is helping you because he also wants to stop lilith and get things back to how they were. But you won't be able to get his blessing until you bring peace to his realm.

So, go up the path and kill the barbarians here, including Gorm, the leader of the barbarians. Talk to Mephisto's wolf form again once they're all down. he'll bless you, and you'll be able to go back through the portal.

When you get back, go to the south entrance of the temple to meet lorath. If you talk to him again, the quest will be done.

Descent Into Flame

Now that Mephisto, Baal, and Diablo have blessed you, you can go into the Temple of the Primes with lorath. head right, climb down, and then jump across the gap to start your journey to the Temple. Follow the path around to the right, killing enemies as you go, until you reach a place where you can climb down.

Get to the level below and follow the path down and around to the left until you reach another place to climb down.

Move forward from this level and take the first right turn to head toward the entrance to the Temple and go inside.

Take a left once you're in the hall of hatred to start making your way through this dungeon to the ritual site. Follow the main path around until you reach a big staircase that leads up to the hall of Destruction.

If you keep going forward from here, you'll reach a big door. It won't open, and something big is standing in front of it. You'll see a demon named Malach, Master of Flame, and you'll have to beat him before you can pass.

Once he's down, go through to keep going to the place of the ritual. At some point, you'll find another set of stairs that lead up to the hall of Terror.

As you move through this next area, you'll reach a spot that looks out over the ritual site. Talk to lorath when you get here. he'll tell you that it looks like you're too late because the ritual has already started, but if you stay in the shadows, he'll deal with Elias. Climb down the wall behind him when he's done to start a cutscene.

After this cutscene, you will fight Brol, The Tyrant King. he is a very hard boss, and you can learn more about how to beat him in the tips below.

❖ how to Beat Brol, the Tyrant King

As soon as you walk into the Altar of Sacrifice, Brol will be ready to fight. he has two big swords that he will use to attack you with big swings. he will also raise the swords above his head for a powerful AOE attack. This will be clear because when he picks them up and puts them back down, he makes a circle on the ground.

When he attacks like this, it's best to try to get around him and behind him. But his swings have a long reach and can still hit you if you're not careful, so you should only give him a couple of hits before moving away.

With the AOE attack, you'll want to move completely out of the circle. But once the circle disappears when he hits his blades, it will take him an extra second to get back up. During this time, you can sneak up behind him quickly to do some damage before he turns around again.

As soon as you hit the first marker, he'll raise a sword into the air, and more enemies will join the fight. During this time, you should pay more attention to them than to Brol, who will be getting ready to try a new move in which he charges straight at you. If he hits you, you'll be stunned and open to more attacks from both the new enemies and Brol, so try to move around the arena to take out the other enemies before focusing on Brol again. If you have a good AOE attack, you can kill a lot of these weaker enemies at once.

Now that they're dead, turn your attention back to Brol. he'll keep using the same attack patterns, so keep doing damage with the same patterns you've used before. As soon as you hit the second marker, he will call down more enemies again, so kill them first while moving around the room to avoid his charge.

This will keep happening until the third marker, at which point he will try another attack. For this one, he will throw his blades up again and then hit the ground three times with them to do a series of small AOE attacks. Small circles on the ground will also be a sign of this. But with this blade attack, the third time he throws them down, he'll be open for a moment, so swoop behind him and hit him before he gets back up.

As soon as you reach the fourth marker, he'll repeat his pattern of calling enemies down in addition to his normal attacks, so stay on your toes while taking them out and avoiding his charge to leave him alone again.

As you get closer to that last marker and the end of his health bar, he will use this move again, so keep avoiding him and dealing damage when you can. Patience will help you a lot right now, because the last parts can feel very intense because there is so much going on.

The quest will be over when he's dead.

loose Threads

Now that you've killed Brol, the Tyrant King, you can go back to lorath and talk to the mysterious woman who was part of the ritual. From the Altar of Sacrifice, go back to where you climbed down to get here and go through the door on the other side.

This will lead you out to the Path of Stray Souls, where you'll find lorath and the woman right outside. She will tell you that she hears a voice in her head if you talk to her. lorath will say that it's Andariel and that he knows something about her. She will say that her name is Taissa and that she thinks Elias may have gone to a palace in the deserts of eastern Kehjistan, which is where he may have gone next. Talk to lorath when she's done talking.

he will tell you to talk to the people in Tarsarak because they know the deserts of Kehjistan better than anyone else. The quest will be done when this scene is over.

Oasis of Memories

On the map below, you can see that Tarsarak is south of where you are.

Once you get there, open the nearby waypoint and then talk to lorath in the middle of town to find out what he knows. he will only have heard rumors about the "endless sandstorm," but he will ask if you can find a guide to help you get through it.

You can talk to a lot of different people in the town square. Talk to each one until you find out that there is an old man near the riverbank who can help you find your way.

Return to lorath and tell him what you've learned. The next thing you need to do is find this old man at the riverbank, which is inside the circle on the map below.

When you get to the bank of the Argentek River, a building in town will be circled on your mini-map. Go inside and talk to the man at the back behind the counter.

he won't be very helpful, so go to the very back door. Unfortunately, the man behind the counter and his friends won't like it and will start attacking you. Take them down, and then go back to the back door.

The old man, whose name is Meshif, is in the next room, on the opposite side from where you came in. Talk to him to find out more about him and how he can help you. The quest will be done once the conversation is over.

Flesh from Bone

Now that you have a guide to help you through the sandstorm, you need to meet lorath and Meshif at the Forsaken Chapel to start your journey. On the map below, you can see where it is.

Talk to lorath inside once you get there and tell him you're ready to start the journey. Then, go outside and talk to Meshif.

It's not easy to get through the sandstorm. You will slowly lose health from the sand, and there will be a lot of enemies to fight, but you can take a break and hide behind some rubble to stay safe and regain health, which is helpful.

Make sure you have plenty of healing potions ready to go, and try to stay as close to Meshif as possible. he moves quickly, and you don't want to lose him in the storm!

You'll get to The Outer Gardens in the end, and the quest will be done.

Beneath the Mask

Talk to Meshif when you get to The Outer Gardens. lorath will tell him to be careful and not talk to anyone while you and he go inside to find Elias. After the talk, you should go to the front door.

A nearby Anointed Noble will stop you from going in right away. If you talk to him, you'll find out that lilith was here recently and that Elias has something called the Sightless Eye. lorath will tell you more about this later. The quest will be done once this conversation is over.

Piercing the Veil

You need to find Elias now that you're inside the palace. lorath will also tell Elias that the Sightless Eye is an old spell that lets him see anywhere, even through time. Keeping this in mind, you should try to take it from him. Start making your way through this dungeon for now.

As you walk through the Noble's Foyer, you'll see several Nobles praising lilith and practicing different spells. They won't pay attention to you because you aren't a threat... yet. At the end, there will be a staircase. Go up it to get to the Inner Gardens.

Move through this area until you get to a big door at the end. Talk to the Anointed Noble standing next to it. he or she will tell you to go inside to meet Elias. After you talk to him, he'll open the door for you.

Elias is in the back of the room. he is standing on Blood Petals that are on the floor. Talk to him to challenge him.

After this short talk, he'll try to get you into a fight with him. This isn't a normal boss fight, though, because his health bar won't be marked. This could mean that this isn't the last fight.

During this fight, he will only shoot things from his staff, which you can avoid to get to him... really a bit too easy for someone like him. Once he's down, you can use the Blood Petals on the floor where he was standing to trigger a cutscene with him and lilith.

When the cutscene is over, you'll find a surprise behind the doors ahead... Elias.

he is still alive and ready for the next fight. In addition to his projectile attack, he will call a demon named Champion of lilith to fight with him. he will also make red pentagrams on the floor, which you can avoid by moving out of red circles. halfway through, he'll also call up another Champion, so deal with that one first before returning to him.

his health bar will stay the same, though, so kill him the same way you did before. Once he's down (for now), go through the door into the room Elias just left. You can listen to the Gospel of the Mother at the shrine in front of you, then keep going to the left through the Inner Gardens.

Keep moving through the Inner Gardens until you reach the halls of the Master, where you'll meet Elias... again. For the first half, he'll use the same attacks as before and call on Skittering Demons and a Champion of lilith to help him. The second half, on the other hand, will be a little bit different.

When his health bar is half gone, he will call two Supplicants to protect him, so you'll have to cut their connection to him to make him vulnerable to attacks. he will also sometimes use explosive AOE attacks on the ground, which can be seen by the red circle around them. Move outside of them to avoid them.

All of this will happen while he is still calling up more enemies, so the fight will be very busy. Once he's down, go into the next area and follow it around until you reach a large room where, you guessed it, Elias is again! This time, though, he'll be ready for a real fight, since his health bar will now have three markers at the top.

During this fight, he will use all of his previous attacks, so use the strategies you've learned from other fights. At the halfway point, he'll call on three Supplicants to protect him, and at the end, he'll call on five. These are the only big changes to his previous attack patterns. Unless something changes, they stay the same until the end.

Talk to lorath once he's down (again, for now). he'll take the Sightless Eye from the pedestal, and then you can go out the door on the left and meet up with Meshif in the Outer Gardens. With this, the quest will be over.

Exhumed Relics

Climb down the wall to get to The Outer Gardens, then go back to Meshif. he won't make it, though, because someone already found him. lorath will tell you to meet him at the Forsaken Chapel after you say goodbye. It's time to look into the Sightless Eye and figure out what to do next.

You'll be taken back to the Chapel after the conversation. Go inside and talk to lorath to find out what happened so you can tell Taissa. This will start a cutscene and end Act 3 of the game.

ACT 4: A GATHERING STORM

Prying the Eye

Talk to Taissa inside the Forsaken Chapel to find out how she is doing.

She will say that she still hears Andariel, but that she can sometimes shut her out. lorath will say that, among other things, he still doesn't know how Andariel fits into Elias and lilith's plan. You'll have to try to use the Sightless Eye to find out what these are.

Get it from the side of the room and put it on the pedestal in the middle. Put it down, then use it by touching it again. This will start a cutscene that will show you where Elias and lilith have gone.

When the vision from the Sightless Eye is over, lorath will come up with a plan and give you a message to give to Donan. The quest will be done when this scene is over.

A Master's Touch

Since you last saw Donan, he has moved. You can find him in Kyovashad at the point on the map below.

When you get there, he will be in the Cathedral of light. Go up there and into the house to talk to him and give him the letter from lorath.

he will say that lorath sent him a plan. lorath wants to lock up lilith with the soulstone, just like Astaroth was. he will also say that the only way for that to work is if the stone is first tuned, which means going back to the horadric Vault.

After this conversation, Donan will also offer you a mount, which will be very helpful on your journey if you haven't already gotten one. The quest will be over at that point.

lost Arts

Go inside the horadric Vault once you reach it to find Donan. he will say that he hasn't even gone inside yet because he's afraid there's someone else there. Open the door to find out who this stranger is...

Neyrelle, it's another friendly face! You can talk to her to wake her up, then introduce her to Donan to start a short scene.

They might not get along well at first, but that's okay. Follow Donan into the Vault for now to open the locked door opposite the one you went through in Act 1.

Go inside and start walking toward his desks from the Gallery. The first one can be found by going straight under the first archway and then turning left under two more archways into a small room with another locked door inside When Donan is sitting at his desk, talk to him to get his notes.

From here, go back out into the hallway, turn left to go down it, then turn right to get back to the main area. From here, you'll need to break down a barrier and get ready to fight some enemies to get to the next desk.

Donan will go into a side room once all of the enemies have been killed. There, you can talk to him to get the next set of notes.

From here, go back into the room where the enemies were and open your map to find the last desk. If you go back to the main room and turn left, you can find the corridor by going down and around. Talk to Donan when he gets there to get the notes, and he'll also take the horadric Amulet next to it.

Now, Donan will open the locked door in this room so you can get back to where Neyrelle is in the Study. Talk to her when you get back there.

She'll tell you that she'll come with you to help you fight lilith, which is great news. When this scene is over, the quest will be done.

A Meeting of the Minds

Now that Donan and Neyrelle are on board to help fight lilith, it's time to go back to the Forsaken Chapel and meet up with lorath and Taissa. Follow the directions on the map below to get back there.

When you get there, Donan and Iorath will be talking to each other, Neyrelle will be on the floor, and Taissa will need to go outside to get some air. Talk to Neyrelle to find out what the plan is for the soulstone.

After a while, Neyrelle will say that the wind is getting stronger and that Taissa can't be found. Go outside the Church to look for her, but stop at the healing Well first to regain your strength.

Talk to Neyrelle outside as the storm gets worse. This will start a short cutscene in which Elias will show up. Because we had already used the Eye, he was able to find us and can now finish the ritual on Taissa to bring Andariel back to life.

This quest will be done when the cutscene is over.

Anguish Incarnate

The first thing to remember about this fight is that the sandstorm has put you in a small arena. If you go into the sandstorm, it will slowly hurt you, so try to fight from inside as much as possible.

During the first part of the fight, Andariel's arms will still be tied together, and she will mostly try to trap you by tying you down. Rune Chains will do this. You'll have to destroy them to get rid of them, and if you get caught in one, it will slow you down. When the Chains appear, a circle on the ground will show you their radius, just like it does for other bosses.

Andariel will also make strong red lines on the ground that will drain your health if you get caught in them, so try to stay away from them when you see them. Sometimes, these lines can branch out from her to cover more ground so keep an eye out for a spot where you can run when the red light comes on.

But this is a good time to hit her from open angles as well. After a few hits, though, she will teleport around and leave red projectiles as she goes. Avoid those and wait for her enemy symbol to show up again on your mini-map to see where she is going next.

When she reaches the first marker, her chains will break and she will fall to the ground. At this point, four sharp pincers will grow out of her back, which she will use to push you away and stab you.

She will also get an extra chain attack to go with the Rune Chains in the arena. Now, she'll use a chain on both her left and right sides as a whip to attack you. You can see her getting ready to hit it on her side, so keep an eye on her sides to know when to get out of the way.

She will keep doing these attacks until the end, so find a good way to avoid her chain whips so you can get behind her and deal damage there.

The quest will be done when she's dead.

Eye of the Storm

After you beat Andariel, go back into the Forsaken Church to see how everyone is doing. When they take down the barrier, they should first talk to lorath to explain what happened.

After the cutscene, talk to lorath again outside to let him know that everyone is ready. After this exchange, both the quest and Act 4 will be done.

ACT 5: SECRETS BARTERED, FATES SOLD

The Path Divided

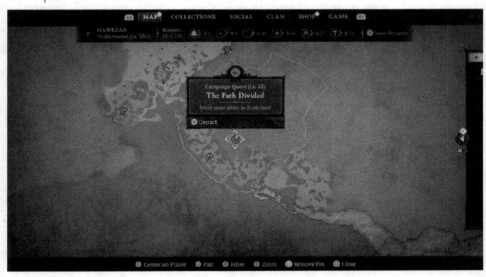

You'll discover Lorath, Taissa, and Neyrelle gathered together in Zarbinzet. Ask Taissa what the strategy is when you speak with her. She'll tell you that Elias's grip on immortality is what's holding you back, and that you need to figure out how to break it.

You'll need to locate a woman named Timue in the swamps in order to accomplish this. She may be able to assist in permanently ending Elias because she is aware of the forces at work here, some of which may be swamp-based.

Now that Donan is aware of the plan, Neyrelle and Lorath will set out on their quest to find her. he will be on the northern side of town, as indicated on the map above, once the conversation is over.

he will say that he needs to concentrate on the soulstone and can't accompany Lorath and Neyrelle.

You will therefore have two options for quests to complete from here. You can either connect with Donan through the quest Secrets of the Zakarum or Lorath and Neyrelle through the quest Tainted Flesh. The quest will be finished once the conversation is over.

Secrets of the Zakarum

On the map below, you can see that Donan is in the Ruins of Rakhat Keep.

Once you get there, you should talk to him. He will say that Mephisto is strong here, which is good for the soulstone. But first you have to figure out how to get into the Keep and open the portcullis for him.

Start by going back to the main path and killing the enemies there. Then, take the left path all the way back until you reach a broken wall that you can climb.

From the top, move forward and up again, then turn around and climb another wall.

At this point, go straight ahead and turn right to find another place to climb down on the right side. From the bottom, follow the path around and jump to a different path to keep going.

Here, turn left and go down the stairs, killing enemies as you go. When you get to the last staircase, it won't work, so you'll have to climb down it to get to the Ruins of Rakhat Keep: Inner Court. You can also open a fast travel point from here.

A Gate Winch is on the other side of the Inner Court from where you entered. Use it to open the gate so that Donan can come in.

Talk to him once he's inside, then follow him to the big door of the Keep and talk to him again. The quest will be done when he opens the way to the Foul Undercrypts.

Entombed hatred

Once you're inside the Foul Undercrypts, go deeper in to find the place where the soulstone can be tuned.

At some point, you'll get to a door that an Ancient Paladin and his guards are standing in front of. Pull them down, and then smash the door.

This will lead you to the Black Tomb of Sankekur, where Donan can make the soulstone work. Start the process by talking to him.

Something will go wrong with it, though, and a Manifestation of Hate will appear. Take it and its guards down, then talk to Donan to find out what happened.

He'll say that what happened with Yorin/Astaroth earlier must have broken it, so it'll need to be fixed. He will tell you to meet him in the village close by when you are ready to start the process.

The quest will be done once this conversation is over.

Tainted Flesh

Lorath and Neyrelle can be found east of Zarbinzet at the point shown on the map below.

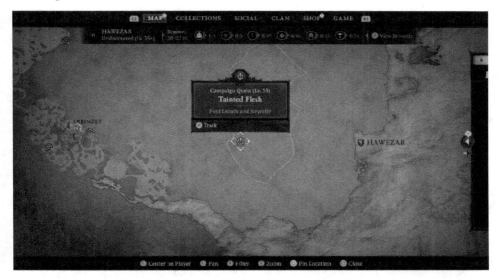

Once you reach the goal, the search area on your map will change into a circle for you to look in. Near the middle, you can find Lorath and Neyrelle. Talk to Lorath when you get there.

He'll tell you that they've had no luck looking for Timue, so you'll have to keep looking together. If you look at your map again, you'll see a new circle where you can look for her.

You can find her on a small piece of land that sticks out from the main area near the southern end of this circle.

Activate the door to go inside and talk to Timue. When you say you are looking for a man named Elias, she will say she has never heard of him. Neyrelle will say that they think he made a deal with the swamp to live forever and that Taissa said she could help. She won't want to help at first, but Neyrelle will be able to change her mind.

Timue will eventually give in and tell you that Elias would have made a deal with the Tree of Whispers if he had made a deal here. You'll need to find the ruins of a town called Yngovani to get there. The way to it will be shown by a sacred incense that is kept in a tower there.

The quest will be done once the conversation is over. You need to find Yngovani right now.

Wrack & Ruin

The map below shows that the search area for Yngovani is quite large, but you'll eventually find it near the centre. As you get closer, the circle on your map will get smaller.

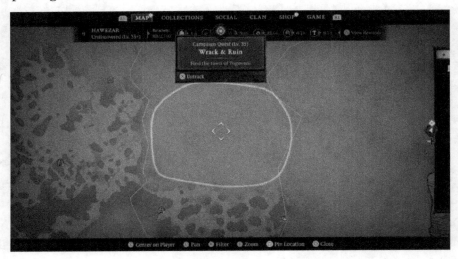

When you get to Yngovani, you'll have to look for the temple. This is on the western side of town. A big stone door in the shape of a snake keeps it closed.

To open this door, you need to find the serpent's eyes, which are out in the swamp. Like before, your map will show you large, circular search areas for each eye.

The right eye is in the circular search area to the right of where you are now on the map. When you go there, look for a Destroyed Serpent Shrine by looking through the bodies of the cultists.

For the left eye, you'll need to go northwest from where you are to the next search area. You have to kill the snakes in the Thieves' Camp and then talk to the Dying Bandit. When he dies, his left eye will fall out, and you can go back to the door.

Put both eyes in the head of the serpent to open the door and finish the quest. You will end up in the Slithering Dark if you do this.

Cold Blood

❖ Cold Blood

You'll need to look for the incense inside the Slithering Dark and bring it back to Lorath and Neyrelle. So, start your journey through here by going through the hole in the wall near the back.

You will get to Mohlon's Nest after going through the Serpentine Passage and the Slithering Depths. The Incense Box is in the back, but it's not easy to get it.

The next boss you'll face is Mohlon, the Snake Queen. This boss's attack patterns and how to beat her are explained below.

❖ How to Defeat Mohlon, Snake Queen

Mohlon is a boss who likes to use poison attacks, so be ready for the room to quickly fill up with poison and, if you can, bring poison elixirs. She also has hatchling eggs all over the place that, when hit, will bring out more snakes and even Nangari Longfangs, so watch where you step and be ready to fight more snake-like enemies in this fight.

She will spit poison at you in a line and swipe at you with her claws and tail when she first attacks. In both cases, you should move out of their way as quickly as you can. She will also call up small poisonous creatures that look like eyes and fire beams at you. Green lines coming out of the beams make them easy to spot, so move quickly to get out of their sight.

Try to kill the other serpents that are fighting with her first so that the room doesn't get too crowded. So it's easier to pay attention to her and not feel too distracted. She won't have any more attacks, either, so keep a pattern of dipping in and out to hurt her or getting some distance so you can shoot at her from afar.

Once she's down, get the Mystic Incense and go back to Yngovani by climbing down the rope that drops.

Talk to Lorath when you get back outside and tell him you have the incense. He'll keep it safe for you while you use it at an altar nearby. The quest will be done once the conversation is over.

Judgement of the Swamp

The altar is at the place marked on the map below.

Talk to Neyrelle when you get there, and then follow her and the others to the Bloodstained Altar. When you get there, kill the enemies before you light the incense.

This will start a cutscene in which a very large snake makes a path through the swamp for you. The quest will be over when it is done.

The Serpentine Path

Now that the snake has made a path for you, you and Neyrelle should start following it.

She will take you to a place in the swamp where you can see the giant snake still moving around. You'll need to follow the serpent's path to get to the Tree of Whispers, so keep going with your group and kill any enemies who get in your way.

You'll eventually get to a place called Sinking Detritus. Neyrelle and Lorath will stop here to look at the snake once more, but soon you'll be attacked by different snake enemies.

If you take them down, Neyrelle will show you an opening under the big snake that leads to the other side. She will try to find a way out by crawling through to the other side.

You'll be attacked again while she looks for a way to move forward. Once all the enemies are dead, Neyrelle will be on top of a broken-down shack and will drop a ladder for you.

Climb up it and then down the other side to keep moving forward. The quest will also be done if you climb down to the other side.

Dirge of the Mire

Talk to Neyrelle once you're past the Sinking Detritus and in a place called the Venom-Drenched Path. When you're done talking, you can keep going through the swamps.

At this point, the path will get hard because you'll need to move down and to the right to keep following the snake around.

You'll get to a spot where it looks like it's hurt. Neyrelle will wonder if this is a sign that it wants you to hurt it, so pull out your weapon and do so.

It will work. The snake will fall into the swamp and make a path for you. Once you're through, keep going.

You will soon reach a group of dead trees when you follow the path. Use your weapon to take them down, and then go on. Follow this path to get to the Voiceless Grove.

Once you get here, follow Lorath to the right, where you'll find the snake blocking your way again. At this point, spirits will sneak up on you and attack. Move around this part of the swamp to get rid of them all, then follow Neyrelle back to the snake, which is now moving to make a path for you.

By going through here, this quest will be done.

The Slow, Beating heart

Once you get to The Swamp of Vanished Souls, talk to Neyrelle. She will bring up the voices that have been talking to you along the way.

When the talk is over, keep going along the path through the swamp. It will lead you right up to the serpent. When you get there, Neyrelle will tell you that this is what she saw before, so you'll have to keep going on top of the serpent's back. This will take you right up to the Tree of Whispers.

As soon as you get there, a cutscene will start. Lorath will tell your group that they are looking for a man named Elias, and the Tree will say that Elias owes them a lot of money. Neyrelle will ask the Tree for help and say that the Tree can get paid if the group can stop him for good.

The Tree will say that Elias wanted to know how to call Lilith, but he stopped along the way to do something else. Unfortunately, the Tree couldn't see that place, but it does know that Elias got there from a coffin past some wrecks on the beach. Talk to Lorath when this conversation is over.

He'll tell you that this coffin might be in the wrecks on the east coast, so that's where you should go next. The quest will be done when this conversation is over. You'll also need to unlock a fast travel point right next to the Tree.

A Cold and Lifeless Shore

Now that the Tree of Whispers has given you more information about Elias, you'll need to meet up with Lorath and Neyrelle somewhere on the eastern coast to find this mysterious coffin that the Tree mentioned. Meet up with Lorath and Neyrelle at the place shown on the map below.

As you get closer to the objective point, the search area on your map will get bigger, but you'll find them in the Sheltered Overhang in the middle of it. Talk to Lorath when you get there.

He'll tell you important facts about Elias's past, like how he became obsessed with Rathma's prophecy, thought he could solve it, and rebelled against Lorath because of it. He'll also tell you that he won't let Elias get away from him again. Now is the time to go out and look for that coffin.

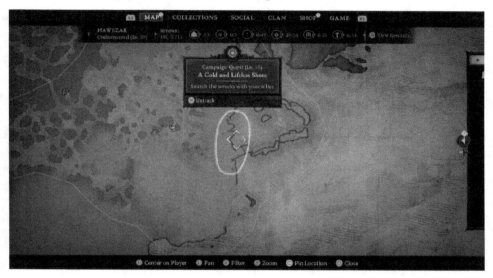

On the map above, the coast is where your search will start. But if you want to narrow it down, go to the land that sticks out into the water near the southern end of the search area.

This will lead you to a large shipwreck on the shore, and if you go to the more open ship on its left side, you can get a better view of the shipwrecks ahead and where the coffin might be. After you talk to your allies about this, the quest will be done.

Picking Through the Bones

Now that you know where to look for the coffin and have a better idea of the shipwrecks, go back to the last one you went into and be ready to fight some enemies. Open the Rotting Door to go deeper into the ship once they're down.

Kill the enemies in this room, and then climb the ladder to the top of the ship, where more enemies are waiting. Once they're down, jump across a gap on your right to the next ship over.

Keep going forward, killing enemies and jumping from ship to ship as you go. You'll eventually come to a locked door that Neyrelle says she can probably open from the other side. She'll leave to do that while you kill the other enemies.

As you do this, though, you will hear a scream coming from the next room. Oh no! Attack the door to break it down and get Neyrelle out of trouble.

When every enemy is dead, talk to Neyrelle. Unfortunately, she will have been infected by one of the enemies from before, so the infected arm will have to be cut off to stop the disease from spreading... Lorath will do the job and keep her company while you finish looking for Elias's secret coffin.

Keep going forward along the path, jumping to other ships and killing enemies who get in your way. At some point, you'll get to the coffin by following this path. When you get there, you can interact with it to start your journey down. Also, this will finish this quest.

Beneath the Wine-Dark Sea

Once you're back on your feet, keep going forward until you find an Echo of Elias you can talk to. After this short cutscene, go right and forward.

When you come to a place where two paths split, take the right one and follow it around and straight ahead until you reach a room with a snake in the middle of the floor and another Echo of Elias standing on top of it.

Talk to him here to find out more about why he's in this underwater temple, and then keep going into the Diaphysis Corridor.

The staircase you need to take will be flooded, though, so break down the pillar to its right to make your own bridge.

To keep following the path through the Diaphysis Corridor, you'll need to hop over this newly built bridge and the rubble in front of it. If you keep going down this main path, you'll come to another fork in the road.

If you go straight ahead instead of to the right, you'll end up in another room with desks and another Echo of Elias. Talk to it to find out what it has to say, then go back to the main path and turn right to keep going.

In the next area, go straight ahead to a path that leads down some stairs and back to the main path. This will eventually lead you to another Echo of Elias which will be the last one.

When you talk to it, you'll find out that the key to his immortality must be deeper in this temple. So, go back out and take the other set of stairs down at that previous fork in the road.

You'll end up in the Corrupted Marrow. Hop over the broken rocks to keep going on the path.

You'll get to a place where you can climb down at some point.

After you do that, turn around and look for another place where you can hop across.

Hop over a few more gaps until you reach an altar with... Elias's finger on it. He put a part of himself here so that he could live forever. You'll have to get it to weaken him, though, so pick it up and keep it close.

If you do that, the temple will fall down, so get ready to get out of there! The place will fall apart around you too quickly for you to get out alive... But don't worry, it's supposed to happen this way.

The quest will be done when the water rises around you.

Fragments of Mortality

After picking up Elias's cut finger and trying to get out of the underwater temple, you'll wake up in the Sheltered Overhang near Lorath and Neyrelle. Talk to Lorath about what you found and ask him what you should do next.

When you're done talking, burn Elias' finger. Neyrelle will be scared when she wakes up, so talk to her.

She'll be shocked by what happened to her arm and afraid that you'll all leave her behind now. Lorath will say that he never thought about it.

When you're ready, they'll meet you at Zakarum Keep, but first you should check on Donan.

The quest will be done when the conversation ends.

Swamp hospitality

You can find Donan in Wejinhani, which is shown on the map below.

Talk to him when you get there. He'll say that the village doesn't have the supplies they need, but the woman he's talking to will say that there's a witch in a nearby tower who can help, so go there. It's just outside of town to the east.

If you go inside the tower, you'll be in for a big surprise when you find out who the witch is... It's Taissa! After her short talk with Donan, you should talk to her and tell her what's going on.

She'll tell you that you can use her tools, but she doesn't have any quicksilver, so you'll have to find a person named Valtha. She is in a place called the "Cinder Wastes."

The quest will be done once this conversation is over.

Witch of the Wastes

With the help of Taissa, you can now work on fixing the soulstone. But you need quicksilver, so you'll need to find a person named Valtha in the Cinder Wastes. Use the search box below to find this person.

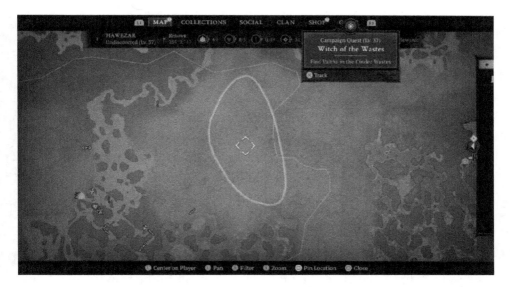

When you go into the search area, you'll find her Hovel near the north end of the circled area. In front, there's a Healing Well.

When you go inside, you'll find a Volatile Cauldron, a Manifesto, and Valtha's Spellbook, which you can use. She won't like it if you look around, though. If you talk to her, you'll find that she just... doesn't like you. So, you should be ready for a fight. Here is a list of Valtha's attacks and how to defend against them.

❖ *How to Defeat Valtha*

Valtha's main attacks won't be poison like many of the enemies in the swamps, but fire instead. Make sure to bring some fire-resistant elixirs to this fight. She will shoot three fireballs from her staff, and she will also rain down explosive fireballs. Many red circles will appear on the ground to show which is which, so just move around the area to stay out of their way.

Because of this, ranged attacks are a good choice against her, and if you have a melee build, swooping in and out to get your shots in is the best way to lower her health.

She will also try to hit you by making a line of fire on the ground. This will look like a straight red line, and all you have to do to avoid it is move away from it. She will also teleport at the end of this attack, so you can time your attacks very well if you know where she will go next. As the fight goes on, she can use this attack multiple times in a row, so keep an eye on where she goes next to stay ahead of her.

When you reach the first mark on her health bar, she will also call in enemies to help her fight (a red pentagram will appear on the ground to show this). These enemies aren't too dangerous, so take care of them first before turning back to her. As you move through the fight up to the second marker, the number of pentagrams will grow up to three to bring in more enemies. Just keep an eye on how crowded the area gets so you can kill them all first.

Once Valtha is dead, pick up the Vial of Purified Quicksilver from the ground and head back to Donan and Taissa. Place the Vial of Purified Quicksilver in the bowl on the table when you get to the tower. Then talk to Taissa and tell her what happened.

The quest will be done once the conversation is over.

Encumbered Mind

Now that the Quicksilver is ready, it's time to fix the soulstone. First, mix the Quicksilver with the other liquids on the left side of the room.

Then, three times, turn the wheel next to Donan.

Then, put the sulphur on the table near the wheel and grind it up.

Donan will now move to the middle of the room to start fixing the damage.

It won't work, though; I don't know why. Taissa will ask to talk to you outside and say that she doesn't think Donan can do the job because he's too preoccupied with what happened with Yorin. She thinks she knows how to fix it, though. All you have to do is go to an old power spot in the swamp.

The quest will be done once this conversation is over.

The Cage of Grief

To start this ritual, you and your allies will need to meet at the Hungering Swamp, which is shown on the map below.

When you get to your goal, go inside the Swamp. On the other side, you have to find the ritual site, which is right in front of you.

Talk to Taissa when you're all inside. She will tell Donan that this is the place where he can face his demons. We just need a few things for the ritual. Donan will have his own things to worry about, but it will be your job to find Maggot Queen Ichor and Yellow Lotus.

The Yellow Lotus is at the northern end of the swamp.

And the Maggot Queen Ichor can be found just to the southwest of the ritual site.

Now that you have those things, go back to the site of the ritual and put both of them in the boiling pot.

Then you need to talk to Taissa. She'll ask you to light the braziers around the room, and then you'll need to talk to Taissa again to drink the tea and start the ritual.

Donan will see a vision of Yorin, but you will have your own experience... with Mephisto. You'll see his fiery portal appear in front of you. Go inside to meet him.

He will take you to a place called the Vision of Travincal and talk a lot about how the Horadrim are holding you back right away. Follow him through this area to keep the conversation going, and talk to him when he stops again.

He'll ask you if you'd rather work with him to stop Lilith than with your allies back home. Talk to him again to tell him that, of course, the answer is no. He'll tell you that if Lilith wins, you'll only have yourself to blame because you didn't work with him.

And now you can leave through the Living Gate and go back to your allies at the Ruined Tower through the portal. This will also finish the quest.

One Step Forward

Talk to Taissa inside the tower to find out what happened with Donan and how he is doing.

Even though it was hard, he made it through and is now ready to fix the soulstone the right way. Talk to him after you've started talking to Taissa.

Repeat the steps from before, but this time mix the quicksilver in the pot on the left, turn the wheel twice over the fire, and then grind the sulphur. Talk to Donan when you're done.

It will work out well! Now that the soulstone is fixed, you can go back to Zakarum Keep and meet up with Lorath and Neyrelle.

On the Precipice

Follow the directions on the map below to get to Zakarum Keep.

Talk to Donan when you get there to make sure everyone is ready to go. Once he's done, everyone should go to the entrance to the Foul Undercrypts.

Once you're inside, head back to the Black Tomb of Sankekur and try to tune the soulstone again.

Talk to Donan to start the rite. All of his, Lorath's, and Neyrelle's attention will be on it, but about halfway through, Taissa will feel that someone else is down here with you all... Elias.

Follow Taissa down the passageway past the Black Tomb to go after Elias. When you reach him, you'll have to fight a boss. Here, we explain how he attacks and how to stop him.

❖ How to Defeat Elias, Fallen Horadrim

In On the Precipice, when you face Elias for the last time, you'll notice that he uses attacks you've seen before. In the past, you would have met Elias a few times during Act 3 during a mission called "Piercing the Veil," but this time he is weak. Now that you have his missing finger, he is no longer immortal, so this is your last chance to stop the Fallen Horadrim.

Like before, he'll call on more enemies to help him in this fight. They'll be different sizes and shapes, and you'll be able to tell by the red pentagrams on the floor. As they show up, try to get rid of them first before going back to Elias. He will also still shoot projectiles at you from his staff, but there will be a lot more of them than before. You can avoid them, though, if you keep moving around him.

After the first marker, he'll throw in another attack that you'll need to watch out for. This is shown on the ground by a bunch of red lines spreading out from his feet. If you get stuck in one of these, your health will go down quickly, so try to stay in the spaces between the red lines or move quickly to the other side before he sets them off.

This attack also comes in many different forms. Sometimes they only cover one side of the area, but as the fight goes on, they will cover almost the whole area. For the second one, just stay in the spaces between the lines to be safe. If you have a ranged weapon, this is a good time to fire as many shots as you can at him. If you don't have any ranged weapons, wait until they disappear before going back in to deal damage. It would also be smart to have a good AOE attack that can chip away at him at these times.

When he has only a tiny bit of health left, a cutscene will start. He'll think you still don't understand that he's immortal, but he'll be shocked when you tell him what you found in the Sunken Temple.

When he hears this, he'll run away from you, and Taissa will start chasing after him again. With this, the quest will be over.

Knee-Deep in Filth

Start following Taissa on the path ahead, past the boss room where you just fought Elias.

At some point, you'll get to the Plaguemarsh, where Taissa is now. If you talk to her and ask where he is, she will say she lost him in the tunnels, but he is now stuck in the swamp. Lorath will catch up to you and help you find Elias in the last few seconds.

When you're done talking, keep moving through the Plaguemarsh until you see Elias slouched against a rock. Talk to Lorath to start a cutscene in which you face Elias and kill him for good.

Talk to Taissa when it's over to find out what comes next. Now that the soulstone is attuned and Elias is gone, she will leave you, but Lorath is no longer there. Neyrelle will say that the Tree of Whispers will now know where Lilith is going because Elias's head is hanging from it, which means Lorath probably went there. Now that you know this, go back to the Tree to look for him.

The quest will be done when this scene is over.

A Chorus of Voices

Talk to Lorath at the Tree of Whispers to find out what happened.

He'll say that he wanted to know where Lilith was going because she's been too far ahead of you for too long, and he finally found out where to find her. He had to promise the Tree his head when he died in order to get the information.

Lorath will then tell them that Lilith has found a way into Hell under Caldeum and is on her way to Mephisto to take his power. Lorath will want to get ready in Tarsarak first, though, before going over there. So, get ready to meet your allies there and get ready for the final battle down below.

When this cutscene is over, the quest and Act 5 will be done.

ACT 6: DANCE OF THE MAKERS

Evil Stirs in Kehjistan

Your allies' location can be found at the spot on the map below, in Tarsarak.

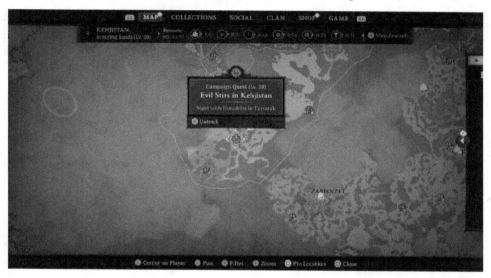

When you arrive in Tarsarak, head inside a building called the Parched Wanderer Inn. However, it'll only be Neyrelle inside. Speak with her to ask where the others are and she'll say that they've already gone to Caldeum since the Knights Penitent are marching on the city and they wanted to follow. Neyrelle, on the other hand, wanted to wait for you.

After this short conversation with her, the quest will be complete. Now it's time to head for Caldeum.

The Jewel of the East

You can find this place to meet up with Lorath and Donan on the map below just west of where you are now.

Talk to Donan when you get to the Caldeum Bazaar. He will tell you that the Knights have already started searching this place for Lilith, who has now opened the gate to Hell below.

When the conversation is over, you'll start looking for Lilith. As shown on the map below, this will show up on your map as a yellow search area west of where you are now. Mark it, and then start your trip through Caldeum.

When you reach the circle, the goal will change to a point that shows where the gate is. If you talk to this Heavy Gate, Inarius will talk to his army, and then Lorath will explain the plan to your allies and you in a cutscene. Inarius, on the other hand, will think your plan is stupid and leave with the soulstone.

You'll need to come up with a new plan now that the soulstone is gone. Talk to Lorath when this scene is over. He will tell you that nothing has changed and that you should just keep going. So, keep going and open the gate to the alley ahead of you.

As you travel through the Residential District of Caldeum, you'll eventually find Prava and some Knights Penitent fighting demons. Kill the enemies near her, and then talk to her.

She won't be on your side, though. Instead, she will help Inarius fight Lilith by going with him. This quest will be done when this scene is over.

The Scouring of Caldeum

After your short talk with Prava, talk to her again and tell her you're also looking for the Hell gate. Lorath will tell you that you'll get there faster if you all go together. She'll agree to let you walk with them, and she'll get everyone to stick with you for the trip.

During this trip, you'll have to lead your allies through Caldeum, so be ready for many waves of enemies.

When you get to the first corner, Prava will yell that an ambush is happening on the rooftops, so you'll need to go up and clear the way.

If you go up the first set of stairs on the left, you'll find a rope at the top that lets you cross to the other side, where the enemies are.

Once everyone is down, take a rope across to the other side from the other side of here. Here, you'll face an even bigger foe: Uznu the Annihilator, the boss. Below, we've broken down how Uznu attacks so you can figure out the best way to stop him.

❖ How to Beat Uznu the Annihilator

You'll meet Uznu as you help your allies clear out the rooftops of the Residential District in Caldeum. He's a big demon with an even bigger sword, which he'll use to attack you with huge blows. As with other bosses who look like this, the best way to avoid getting hit by the sword during these attacks is to move around or under him to his opposite side.

He also breathes fire, so elixirs that protect against fire will be helpful. Most of the time, his fire will only reach a small area around him, as shown in the picture above by the flaming line on the ground. If you move back or to the other side of where his head starts to breathe fire, you'll be safe.

But, unfortunately, these lines will be around for a long time (not for the whole fight, thank goodness, but for a long time). They will make it harder for you to move around him, so you'll need to keep an eye on the ground as you move to hurt him. Since you're fighting in a long area, it's best to move up and down so he can't trap you in a small circle.

When it comes to fire-based attacks, he will also fly up and breathe fire into the air to make little projectiles after the first mark on his health bar. These will fall down in different places around you, as shown above by the red circles that appear on the ground. So, when they show up, make sure to move out of the circles and wait until they stop before you start attacking again.

Once he's down, take your rewards and go down the stairs and two ladders in front of you to meet up with your opponents.

A Knight will break down the wall in front of you so you can keep going. At some point, you'll come to a locked gate that you'll need to open for them. Before you do that, talk to Lorath and your allies.

Donan will say that he doesn't trust Prava, but Lorath will tell him that for now, it's best to have their army behind them. You both want the same thing after all. When the cutscene is over, you'll need to climb the ladder behind Lorath to get to the winch and open the gate so everyone can get through.

The gate will fall down behind everyone, so you'll have to find a different way to get around. This quest will be finished when you do this.

The Walls Shake

From the gate winch, you need to go backward to get to the area circled on the map below.

At some point, the path will lead you to a place called the Foul Cistern. This is where you'll find another boss, and it's a nasty one. This is Duriel, Lord of Pain, another of Lilith's lesser evils that she has called forth.

❖ How to Defeat Duriel, Lord of Pain

Like Mohlon, the Snake Queen from Act 5, Duriel's boss arena will be surrounded by eggs that, when hit, will hatch into Plague Maggots. When a lot of them hatch at once, the area can feel really overwhelming, so you'll want to move slowly as you avoid Duriel's attacks and try to kill them first.

If you have a good area-of-effect attack, you can trap a group of enemies together and kill them all at once. Duriel also likes to dig, so he will dig holes on different sides of the arena while the fight is going on. Because of this, you'll only be able to fire a few shots at a time, so be ready to take your time with this fight.

Now, Duriel is a big creature that looks like a maggot. He has two big pincers on his front that he will use to stab you, so try not to fight in front of him. Moving under and around him is a great way to get a few hits in before moving away.

He can also use his pincers to attack by making a couple of swipes and then slamming both of them down at once. If you're not careful, this can do a lot of damage to you, so try to have your dodge ready so you can quickly move out of the way when they lift up.

Duriel also has a lot of poison attacks, so keep elixirs on hand to protect yourself from poison. His big trick is to spit a line of poison from his stomach at you. Because his stomach is so big and full of teeth, you'll be able to tell when he's getting ready to take off.

Duriel's stomach mouth is another good reason why it's better to deal damage to him from behind instead of in front of him: he can eat you. He will eat you and then spit you out after doing a lot of poison damage to you.

When the battle is over, take your rewards and keep going to the Imperial Palace. When this fight is over, the quest will also be done.

Turning the Tide

When you leave the boss arena, go to the right and up some rubble. Follow this to reach the Imperial Palace.

Once you get inside, Neyrelle will be waiting for you. Follow her back to the Imperial Library to meet up with the rest of your group, and then talk to Lorath.

He will tell them that they now know where to go next: the Cathedral of Hatred. There's no doubt you'll find Lilith there. Now get ready for your trip to Hell.

Interact with the Blood Petals on the floor before you go through the Gates of Hell. You'll see a short cutscene with Lilith, and then you can talk to Neyrelle. Go through the Gates when everyone is ready. With this, the quest will be over.

Essence of Hatred

As you go deeper into Hell to find Inarius' army, you will meet a lot of enemies. You should expect to fight a lot along the way.

When you get to the Burning Overpass, you'll see the bodies of people you know. Here is where the real battle between Inarius and Lilith's armies happened. It looks like there aren't many survivors, but Prava is still holding on in this area. If you talk to her, you'll find that she has the soulstone with her as well. This means that you can stick to your original plan.

Talk to her to find out where Inarius is. She will say that he went to the Spire to find Lilith and that she had the soulstone on her the whole time you were helping her in Caldeum. She will be very upset that you gave it back, but there's nothing you can do now.

Donan will give her a drink that will help her get back to Caldeum for now. When this scene is over, the quest will be done.

In Desolation's Wake

After you talk to Prava, you should talk to Donan. He'll tell you and the others that you need to be careful as you go deeper into Hell, especially now that you're all on your own.

Move up the Burning Overpass and into The Desolation Fields. Near the end of this area, enemies will jump out of the sky and attack you. Climb up a wall near where your allies are making a shield to get to the enemies up high

Here, you'll meet Ninsa, the Blight of Hatred, who is an enemy. Here, we'll talk about Ninsa's attack patterns and how to beat her as a boss. Keep in mind that she will go away during this fight and then come back later. But if she does come back, your allies will be there to help you fight her.

❖ *How to Beat Ninsa, Blight of Hatred*

Ninsa, Blight of Hatred is a boss who, when first met, puts up a barrier to protect herself. To get rid of this, you'll need to kill the enemies around her that are feeding it, which you can tell by the red lines that connect them to the sphere around her. During this time, she will also call in more enemies to fight you. If you have a good area-of-effect attack, drop this while you kill the Soul Burners to protect her.

When it comes to her main attacks, she will fire blue projectiles at you and also try to hit you with fireballs. Red circles on the ground are a good way to find these.

When she comes back in the Searing Expanse, her attacks will be mostly the same, but you will have help from your allies. This will help you stay safe when she throws fireballs at you because Donan and Lorath will form a shield around you.

The first time she runs away, you can get back to your allies by climbing back down the wall you used to get up. Help them kill the last of their enemies, and then keep going through the Realm of Hatred.

At some point, you'll run into a wall of fire, which Neyrelle will put out. As you move forward, you will get to another. But at this point, you should talk to Lorath. Neyrelle will offer to break down the wall, but Ninsa will come back, destroy the bridge ahead, and call a demon named Karum to fight for her. We've broken down Karum, the Hound of Hatred's attacks below so that you can easily kill him.

❖ *How to Beat Karum, Hound of Hatred*

Karum is like the other demons you've fought. He has a big sword that he'll swing and slam at you during the fight. Your allies will help you in this battle, so you won't be alone. Unfortunately, Karum won't be alone either, because Ninsa will drop fireballs around you to help him. Before the plane lands, red circles will appear on the ground to show where these are.

Karum can also shoot lines of fire from under him that go in different directions. These will roll away from his feet, but you can see where they will go. This will help you figure out what to do next.

When running away from a big demon like him, it helps to go under him or run in a circle around him. He moves slowly because he is so big, so you have time to get around him. Since he mostly uses his sword, ranged attacks are very helpful. However, melee users can dodge under him to get behind him and deal damage. Just make sure to get some space before going back in.

Once he's down, you'll have to find a different way in. You can jump into the Twisted Pathway through a gap to the right of where Neyrelle put out the second wall of fire.

At some point, Ninsa will come back to the Searing Expanse to finish the fight. During this fight, your allies will be there to help you, which will be useful because her attacks will be more dangerous than they were before. As she throws many fireballs at you, Donan and Lorath will make a barrier to protect you all.

Her attacks will stay the same, except that they will happen more often. She will still shoot blue arrows, drop fireballs from the sky, and call on many enemies to help her. Try to get rid of the other enemies before going back to fight her. At each point on her health bar, she will rain fire on you all. This is when you should run for cover behind Donan and Lorath.

Talk to Lorath once she's down for good. Everyone's moment of peace will be cut short when another boss joins the fight... It's a story you may have heard before. Ashava, the Pestilent, will let you know she's there. If you've been exploring the open world already, you may have already met her. We've written down how to beat her so you can move on.

❖ How to Beat Ashava

Ashava will never be immune to damage, so bring poison elixirs, which you can make in town, because there will be a lot of poison. During this fight, though, your allies will help you in very helpful ways. During the fight, they'll keep Ashava in a trap, which basically knocks her out, so you can do as much damage as you can before she gets back up.

Her first attack is a big sweep in a circle around where she is standing. This can be a nightmare for people who use ranged weapons. If you are in this area, you are likely to die. If you avoid the swipe, watch out for her for a second as she tries to get you again. If you use melee attacks, you can avoid damage by moving closer to Ashava as her talons get closer to you. Continue DPS as normal.

Her second big attack is a swipe, but this time she uses both of her talons to start in front of her and end behind her. Getting hit by this attack will poison you to the point where you are almost dead.

Ashava can lunge forward with her head and eat you if you stand in front of her. This attack does a lot of damage and could kill you, so stay away from her mouth.

The other two ways she will attack are not as dangerous as the first two, but they should still be avoided. Ashava can shoot poison from her mouth that pools all over the battlefield and makes it hard to move as the battle goes on. She also has a slam attack that hits a large area and is shown by a circle.

Once she's out of the way, you can get your rewards and the quest will be done.

Light Extinguished

Talk to Lorath to find out how everyone is doing now that Ashava is down. Then go through the doorway in front of you to get into the Molten Span.

This will take you to the Spire of Torment, where you can interact with Blood Petals. This will start an exciting cutscene that shows you what happened down here before.

When the cutscene is over, talk to Neyrelle about what you saw and then follow Lorath.

Lilith won't be there when you get to the last place she was, but Lorath will have an idea. He brought the Sightless Eye with him and will set it up so you can look inside to find out where she is.

After he puts it down, you can interact with it to start a scene with your allies. During this time, though, Donan will get lost because the Pillar of Demons will draw his attention away... one will try to hurt him.

After this, a number of dead bodies will start to fall from the pillars. Take them out and destroy the pillars, then talk to Donan. He'll say that he's fine and that Lorath is right, that the Eye is the best way to find Lilith.

When this scene is over, the quest will be done.

The Blind Eye

Talk to the Sightless Eye again to find out where Lilith is.

Spying on her won't be easy, though, because she'll notice you right away. When she does, you'll be thrown into a nightmare world from which you'll have to find a way out.

As you move through here, Lilith will try to convince you that she's right, while you see memories of places you've been and people you've met.

At some point, you'll get to Lilith's Altar. When you talk to it, Lilith will ask you to help her destroy Mephisto. Of course, you'll tell her no, which she won't like.

She will send you a number of enemies that you will have to beat. She will also summon Hellbinders to hold you down as more enemies come.

Mephisto and his fiery portal will help you when things seem hopeless. You can get out of this area and out of this nightmare by jumping through it.

He'll tell you to go through the gateway, so keep going into the cave where you started this whole trip and talk to the campfire on the other side.

This will take you to a cutscene where Mephisto will let you know he's there. He'll say he's here to set you free and give you his blessing to help you get out of here.

After the cutscene, jump off the edge of the cliff to start your way out. Lilith will try to block your way by destroying the path, and she will also call Genbar, the Shrine-Keeper, Brol, the Tyrant King, Elias, the Fallen Horadrim, Airidah, the Keeper of the Dead, and Astaroth, all bosses you've already fought.

Be careful in all of these fights. And if you need more help, be sure to check out our guides for each boss.

At some point, the Sightless Eye will be floating in the air. Use it to get out of this nightmare and get back to your friends. If you do that, the quest will also be done.

What Lies Ahead

Talk to Neyrelle now that you've escaped Lilith's nightmare through the Sightless Eye. She'll be crying, and Donan won't have a good time of it.

This will start a scene where you and your allies talk to each other.

When the cutscene is over, Neyrelle will be down a path from where you are, as shown on the map below.

When you get there, talk to her. Not long after that, Mephisto's portal and him will appear. Neyrelle will be shocked to find out that you trusted a Prime Evil, but she will decide to follow you through the portal to the Cathedral of Hatred. When the cutscene is over, you can go through the portal.

Start walking towards the Cathedral from the other side. Along the way, Neyrelle will suggest putting Mephisto in the stone instead of Lilith because something doesn't feel right about how helpful he is and he is the worse of the two evils.

You'll eventually reach the Throne of Hatred, where you can decide what to do with the soulstone. Talk to Neyrelle to find out what you should do next.

In the end, you'll both decide to seal the gates behind you and leave Mephisto trapped in the stone and Lilith here in Hell.

Then, Neyrelle will stab the soulstone into Mephisto, and you'll tell her it's time to kill Lilith for good. Lilith will go into the Cathedral as she leaves through the portal. Now it's time for the big battle at the end.

A few things you should know before this fight: Make sure you are close to the level you should be to fight her. She comes in at level 45, so being there or close to it will help. You should also bring elixirs with you. Fire resistance in particular. She has a number of attacks that use fire, so it's good to have them ready. It's also because she will try to overwhelm you many times during these fights, so you'll want to have extra defences ready.

In the same way, AOE attacks will also be very helpful. She will keep calling more enemies as the fight goes on, so being able to take them out in groups will keep it from getting too hard.

❖ *How to Beat Lilith, Creator of Sanctuary*

As you can see in the picture below, one of Lilith's first attacks will be to scratch at the ground around you, causing cracks that will spread flames. Thanks to how far apart these claw marks are, you can easily walk between them or quickly move out of the way when you see one coming.

Use a ranged weapon or an attack that affects a large area while you move around these attacks. If you have a close-range weapon, try to hit her where the claw marks are to get close to her. They don't last long, so just keep an eye out for where they'll form next so you don't get caught in them.

She will also use her wings to hit you very hard. If you're close to her, it might be harder to avoid these shots, so it's best to move back and get some distance while she whips them around.

She will also use her wings to push up sharp rocks in a wave, as well as to swipe at you. When she moves, these spikes will ripple out from under her in one direction, so move to the side when you see them coming.

When you get close to the second mark on her health bar, she will jump up and land in the middle of the arena. From here, she will jump into the air and make red swirls on the ground that will call more enemies to help her fight. There will be a lot of different ones to go through. Make sure to get rid of all of them first before you turn back to her. Again, if you have good AOE attacks and can get everyone close together, they will work great here.

During this time, Lilith will keep doing her usual swipes and spikes, so you'll have to stay on your toes to avoid them while you kill these enemies.

When the big group of enemies is defeated, she will sometimes still call on other enemies (usually Succubus) to help her fight. When she does, turn your attention to them before going back to her so you don't get too busy.

As her health bar gets close to the middle, her claw attack will also change.

She'll start making them into a lattice pattern instead of just straight lines, so you'll need to find safe places between the lines to hide while they run their course.

At the third mark on her health bar, she'll head back to the centre of the arena to call more enemies. This time, though, she'll jump into the air and slam down with spikes coming out from under her. A big red circle on the ground will give you time to figure out where this attack will land. Make sure to avoid her by getting out of the way.

She will keep doing this attack along with her other attacks all the way to the end. But Lilith's story isn't really over...

Her body will sink into the floor, and a red pool will form in the middle of the arena... Lilith, the Daughter of Hate, will come out of it.

❖ *How to Beat Lilith, Daughter of Hatred*

The Daughter of Hatred is different from the last boss fight because she has new tricks. She will start this fight by putting four piles of a red substance around the arena. You'll move more slowly if you step in one of these, and she'll keep making more as the fight goes on, so do your best to avoid them as you deal damage to her.

She will also try to stab you with her tail and hit you with her wings a lot. Not only that, but she has a pretty powerful attack where she swipes both wings at you and then stabs down on top of you. If you get hit by that attack, it can do a lot of damage to your health. To avoid it, try to move backward, get some distance, or go around the sides of her.

If you're using a close-range weapon, try to move under her and hit her from behind before she flies away. And if you have a gun with a long range, use the distance to your advantage.

The arena will be part of her next big attack. She will jump into the air, fly over a part of the arena, and then land. The part she'll fly over will actually catch fire, and if you get caught in it, your health will go down a lot. In this case, try to figure out where she's going and run that way.

After the first marker, she will do the same thing, but on the other side she will build a wall. Stay away from this barrier at all costs, because it will eventually break down that part of the arena (and you can die if you're on the wrong side of it), making it even harder to move around.

Even worse, the red stuff around the arena will also shoot projectiles at you during this time, so you'll also have to avoid those. If you're using a ranged weapon, this is a great time to shoot at her, but if you're using a melee weapon, it's best to wait until that part of the arena collapses. But it gives you more time to get out of the way of the projectiles, which is good.

As soon as the floor starts to fall apart, Lilith will go back to the middle of the arena for a slam attack. This one is tricky because she'll make a vortex that slows you down. To avoid damage, you'll need to get out of its range as quickly as you can.

These attacks will keep going as long as the fight does, and Lilith will keep breaking down the arena's edges. As the fight draws to a close, you'll need to be patient while dealing damage to her because you'll have less room to move around.

When she is on the ground, a cutscene will start. You've done it! You've defeated Lilith. Get your rewards and go back to Lorath through the portal that appears.

Talk to him and tell him that Lilith is gone and that you and Neyrelle decided to put Mephisto in the soulstone instead. He'll get it and ask where the stone is now, which is a great question... what happened to Neyrelle?

She must have already gone to the Chapel, so you'll have to go there and look for her. But first, you have to get Donan out of here and shut the gates to Hell.

This will finish the quest and Diablo 4's Act 6.

EPILOGUE: FROM THE WOUND SPILLED

Promises

Go into the Chapel and check to see if Neyrelle is there.

Lorath will say that she is missing. Talk to him and tell him you think she might have gone back to the Horadric Vault. He will tell you to check there next time, so go back outside. Out there, you'll meet some unhappy people, which is a shame...

Iosef is a member of the Knights Penitent. When you talk to him, he'll say that they're here for Lorath. If he doesn't want to go with them, though, they'll start a fight.

After you beat them, pick up Prava's Decree, which they dropped. Here, you can find out how Prava thought the Horadrim brought evil into the world, which is why the Knights Penitent were looking for Lorath.

When you talk to Lorath again after the fight, he'll tell you that he's going to bury Donan and that you should go to the Vault to find Neyrelle.

The quest will be done when the cutscene is over.

A Heavy Burden

You should go to the Horadric Vault. You won't find Neyrelle there, but there will be a letter for you on a table in the middle of the room. Interact with it to get it, then get ready to take it back to Lorath.

With this, the quest will be over.

Legacy of the Horadrim

Lorath is to the left of Firebreak Manor, where Donan is being buried.

Talk to him to give him the letter. He will be able to read it because it is written in Horadric code. This will start a cutscene that tells you where she is now.

The quest will be done when it's over. You have now finished the main storyline of Diablo 4.

ꙮSIDE QUESTSꙮ

FRACTURED PEAKS SIDE QUESTS

Secret of the Spring

On the Kylsik Plateau, just north of the town of Kyovashad (as shown on the map above), you can find a Discarded Note on the ground. This says: if you pick it up.

"Beacon of warmth in winter's embrace, patience is rewarded by nature's own grace."

This will start a side quest called "Secret of the Spring." To keep going with it, go to the blue circle on your map, which is northeast of where you are right now.

Once you get there, you'll have to kill a few enemies before finding a small spring. here's where you'll need to figure out the note's puzzle.

Since it says "Patience is rewarded," you'll need to spin your Emote wheel until you find the "Wait" Emote, which best represents "patience."

You will get treasure if you use it while facing the spring. You will also get +20 Fractured Peaks Renown, 2,912 XP, and 720 Gold when you finish this side quest.

Unwritten End

When you find the Merchant's ledger, which is just southeast of Kyovashad at the location shown on the map below, you'll be told to bring it back to Zalan Coste in Margrave.

Go back to Margrave and give the ledger to him. he'll tell you about it briefly and then the quest will be over. You'll get +20 Fractured Peaks Renown, 1,932 XP, 520 Gold, and a Cache when you're done.

Raising Spirits

Go to Kyovashad and find Guard Boza. Ask her how the city guard is doing. She says that all she wants is for you to cheer for the new guards because she doesn't want to seem weak. No problem!

Your map will show a small blue circle where you can go to cheer on the training militia. This is a good way to learn how the Emote wheel works, so open it up and tab to the left to choose "Cheer."

You can then go back to Guard Boza to finish the Side Quest and get 1,596 XP, 440 Gold, and a herb Cache.

Menestad Coffers

This quest is a little to the left of the Fast Travel point to Kyovashad. Talk to Kudomyla the Tithe Collector to get it going.

She will tell you that a Monk named Bozan hasn't come back from a delivery to Menestad yet, and she wants you to go look for him. So, open your map and look for the blue circle in the northwest. This is where you should start your trip.

he will be in the north part of the circle, past a bridge that you will cross on the main road. Talk to him when you get there, and he'll tell you that his guard turned against him. he won't be able to make it the rest of the way with the Tithing Demands, so you'll have to finish the journey for him.

Go to the Strongbox next to him to get the goods, then head to Telgun the Merchant lord, who is a little to the left of where you are now in Menestad when you look at a map. You will get 1,596 XP, 440 Gold, and a Salvage Cache when you finish the quest.

Malady of the Soul

Sister Octavia needs help in Kyovashad, and you can find her there. She will tell you that she needs your help to get rid of a demon from a young boy and that you should follow her into the nearby cellar.

Talk to Sister Octavia again when you get there. She will ask you to take her holy chalice and put it in front of the boy who is possessed while she reads from her prayer book. So go into the room and put the holy chalice there.

Sister Octavia will come into the room after she does this. Talk to her again to get the exorcism started.

The boy's demon will call on Carvers for you to fight, and then the demon will show up himself. The boy will be saved if you kill Xul'goth.

After that, go outside and talk to Sister Octavia. She will tell you that you did a good job and that she would be happy to have your help again. This will finish the quest and give you 7,680 Experience Points, 1,100 Gold, and a herb Cache.

The Sealed Door

You can find a beggar on the side of the road on the eastern side of town. You can talk to him and offer him money, but he won't take it. Instead, he'll tell you that he has a bad feeling something bad is going to happen north of here and that a door is in danger.

he will say that it was sealed for a reason and that some animals are trying to open it. he'll ask for your help to stop them and keep the door shut, so start your journey by going to the blue circle that's circled in red below.

You'll have to fight off many enemies as you search this area, but you'll find the door in the northeast corner of the circle. The name for it is the hoary Gate.

here, a Death Priest is trying to open the door. When you kill it, the quest will be done and you'll get 8,184 XP, 920 Gold, and a leather Cache.

The Cleansing Flame

To start this side quest, you'll need to talk to Priest Matvey near the pyre in the middle of town. he'll ask if you can light a brazier to keep bad things from coming from Margrave, so open your map, find the marker, and head over there.

Once you get there, you'll have to light the Ritual Brazier to start the ritual. After that, you'll have to kill different enemies to clean up the area.

Return to Priest Matvey when you're done to finish the quest. You'll get 2,080 XP, 450 Gold, and a Murmuring Cache.

A Cold Faith

In the open world of Fractured Peaks, you might find a Pilgrim's Journal and his dead body in the spot below. When you pick up this journal, a side quest called "A Cold Faith" will start. For this quest, you have to give this journal back to Priest Matvey in the nearby town of Margrave.

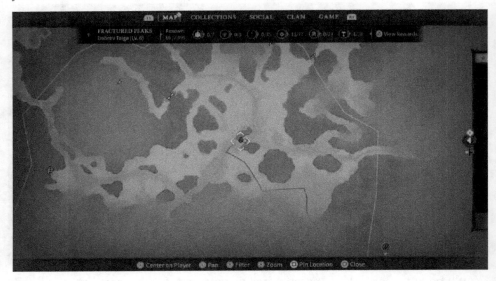

When you get to Margrave, go to the person with the blue marker on top of his head. This is Matvey the Priest. Tell him you found the body of a pilgrim from Margrave when you talk to him. he will say that it's too bad he didn't finish his pilgrimage, and that will be the end of the quest.

You'll get +20 Fractured Peaks Renown, 240 Gold, 204 XP, and a Cache when you finish this quest.

Bound by Blood

You can hear a man arguing with some other people in the town of Margrave If you ask him what's going on, he'll say that some local hunters went with his brother, Perithan, to guide some merchants through the mountain, but they were attacked by bandits. Iacthan doesn't believe that what the hunters say about Perithan is true. he will ask if you will be his bodyguard while he looks for Perithan. If you say yes, the quest will start.

Before you leave, he'll ask you to check with Priest Matvey, Guard Cvetko, and Meridan to see if he's already back. No one has seen him around lately, so go to the place where the merchants were ambushed to find out what happened.

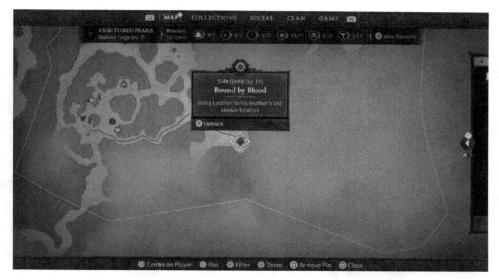

Once you get there, look for clues. Soon it will be clear that Perithan did join the bandits, so take the path into the Western Tunnel to look for him and find where the bandits are hiding. From here, you can get to the Cutthroat's Escape.

If you keep going through this tunnel, you'll end up in a small boss room where you'll find Perithan in a corner and have to fight the Outlaw Sharpshooter. This mini-boss shoots projectiles from their crossbow, makes red pools that can drain your health, and sets up bear traps, so you'll have to move around while taking your shots.

Talk to Perithan once they're dead to finish the quest. You'll get 3,641 XP, 540 Gold, and a Cache.

legacies of light's Watch

You'll see a man on the ground in the town of Margrave who looks like he's in pain. If you talk to him, you'll find out that his name is Zalan Coste. he will say that he went to the light's Watch outpost because his mother was stationed there and he is trying to find some lost records, but the place is full of enemies. So he will ask you for help.

After the conversation, go to the map point to look for the Archivist's Journals.

As soon as you get there, you'll run into enemies, so be ready to fight big waves of them. Start moving through the Outpost and clearing it out while you look for the three Archivist's Journals you need.

Once you have all three, you can finish the quest by going back to Zalan. You'll get +20 Fractured Peaks Renown, 3,192 XP, 550 Gold, and a Salvage Cache for doing this.

Unyielding Flesh

Talk to Krystyna in the town of Yelesna to get started on this quest. She will say that her husband just up and left, but she heard him talking to another woman before he left. She'll ask if you can help her find him, so go to the circle marked in blue on your map to start looking.

At some point, you'll find him in... a very bad situation. Krystyna will ask you to find the woman who did this to him, so go to the blue circle on the map, which is where she is.

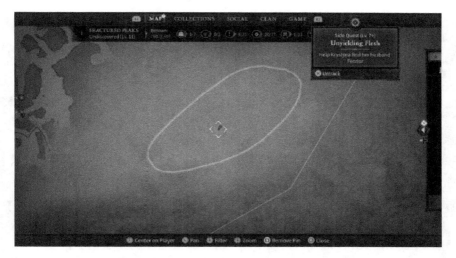

This woman is actually a demon in disguise, and she doesn't want you to get in the way of her plans. So we need to fight. Get rid of her, then go back to Krystyna.

She will tell you that if you want a reward, you should take the Blood-Barbed Blade, a Rare Dagger, from his chest. When you finish the quest, you'll also get +20 Fractured Peaks Renown, 1,932 XP, and 520 Gold.

Ravenous Dead

An alchemist in Yelesna named Olesia will ask you to get her 15 Ghoul hearts. You can find these in the blue circle on the map that is circled in yellow, which is just to the right of the town.

When you have everything, you need to go back to her to finish the quest. You'll get +20 Fractured Peaks Renown, 3,520 XP, 600 Gold, and a herb Cache for doing this.

Traveler's Prayer

The Pilgrim's letter is on a table when you walk into The hog's head. To start this quest, pick it up and read it. It'll say:

"I started my pilgrimage from Yelesna. I thanked a shrine on the side of the road and got a blessing for my trip."

For this side quest, you can go to the shrine the Pilgrim talks about and give thanks to see what you might get in return.

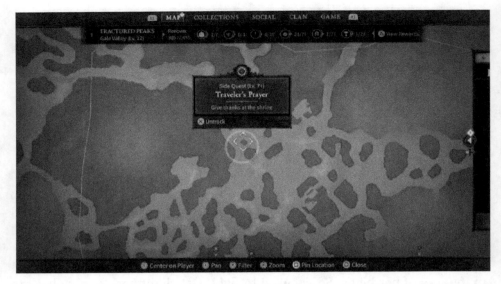

Go to the circled area on your map and follow the road until you see a shrine at the end. When you do, say "Thanks" from the Emote wheel, and Pilgrim's Supplies will drop for you to take. When you finish the quest, you'll also get +20 Fractured Peaks Renown, 1,932 XP, and 520 Gold.

Gory Display

You can start this side quest by picking up a Warrior's Chain on the ground after defeating a group of enemies at the location below.

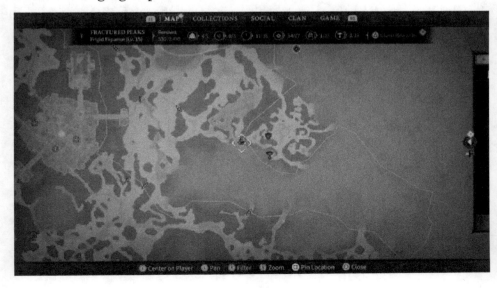

Bring this Chain back to the Bear Tribe Refuge, which is at the blue marker below, and tell them what happened there.

Talk to Sena about the trap when you get to the Refuge. This will finish the side quest and give you +20 Fractured Peaks Renown, 2,496 XP, 640 Gold, and a Cache.

Shattered Tribute

Ask Sena if you can talk to the Chieftain while you are in the Bear Tribe Refuge. She will say that you have to work for an audience, so you'll have to find the khazra from the Ice Clan who attacked her tribe earlier.

To do this, you'll need to find 25 Ice Clan Bones. So, go to the place marked on your map to start hunting down and collecting from these enemies.

When you have everything, take it all back to Sena to finish this quest. You'll get +20 Fractured Peaks Renown, 5,400 XP, 850 Gold, and a leather Cache for doing this.

The Beast's Challenge

Talk to Greganoch about the trophies behind him in the village. he'll say that he's missing one: Kauller the Collector, a goatman. It hunts north of the Refuge, and he'll ask you to go find him. So, on your map, find the blue circle with a white outline to start looking for him.

Kauller is in Sinner's Pass, just north of Bear Tribe Refuge. When you find him, you'll have to fight him. he's a pretty tough enemy, so it's important to be at the right level for this quest. You can go back to Bear Tribe Refuge once he's down.

Talk to Greganoch when you get there, and then put the head on the wall with the other trophies. You'll get +20 Fractured Peaks Renown, 5,400 XP, 850 Gold, and a Salvage Cache when you finish this quest.

Gold Well Spent

When you are in Menestad, you will meet a man named Meros who needs help. If you ask him what he wants, he will say that a man named luskas took advantage of a deal he made, and he wants you to go get the Payment of Gemstones back for him. So, on your map, go to the circle with the arrow to start your search.

When you get there, luskas The Cold-hearted will meet you and be ready to fight.

Take him out and get the Payment of Gemstones to give to Meros.

Give him the Payment of Gemstones to finish the quest. You'll get +20 Fractured Peaks Renown, 3,864 XP, 650 Gold, and a herb Cache for doing this.

⊱DUNGEONS⊰

FRACTURED PEAKS DUNGEONS

Anica's Claim

❖ *location of Anica's Claim*

Anica's Claim is in the town of Malnok and can only be reached after the stronghold has been cleared. This town can be found east of Kyovashad.

❖ *Anica's Claim Dungeon*

This dungeon doesn't have any bosses, but like other dungeons, you should make sure you're ready before going in because the number of monsters might catch you by surprise. The hallways here are pretty wide, so as long as you keep an eye on where you are, you should be fine.

Most of the enemies here will be goatmen, so be ready to dodge the Marauders' axes if you don't want to get knocked down. The dungeon's first goal is to get Animus from Animus Carriers. These carriers are elite monsters, and the words "Animus Carrier" will be written next to their names to show this.

They also have a skull icon on the minimap and dungeon map, so you can find them that way. After you kill them, you need to walk over to the violet fogs they leave behind because that's where the animus is. Once you have them all, go to the urn in front of the locked gate and pour them in there to open the gate.

Next, you need to find the Ancients Statue and put it back on the pedestal. Because of this, you'll have to look for it all over the second area. A lot of monsters will keep an eye on it. Always check your minimap to see where the icon for it is.

After you put the Frozen heart back on the pedestal, you can do something with it. After you talk to them, monsters will appear. If you kill them all, the elite monster hiding inside the Frozen heart will be shown. If you kill it, the dungeon will be empty.

Black Asylum

❖ *Where is Black Asylum?*

The area of Fractured Peaks called "Frigid Expanse" is where Black Asylum is. Northeast of Kyovashad is where this is.

❖ *Black Asylum Dungeon*

Even though there isn't a boss in the dungeon, there will still be a lot to do there. Still, it will be hard because there are so many different kinds of mobs and there are so many of them. Be careful around Wraiths and their red beams of lightning. They can only cast this spell if there is another enemy nearby, so you'll want to get rid of the mobs or the wraith first.

In the first part of the dungeon, you'll have to find and turn on Gate Winches. With these winches, you can open the locked gate to the next part of the dungeon. The mobs that follow you and the large size of the dungeon can make it take a long time to find the winches. You can ignore the mob and only fight when you have to, which will make this phase go faster.

You have to kill every monster in the area in the second part of the dungeon. This is another job that takes a lot of time and can be hard. This is because some of the monsters are inside cells, where they are easy to miss. Because of this, you should pay attention to your environment and the minimap. Make sure it doesn't have any red dots.

Also, it seems like you don't really need to "slay all enemies" in the area, which is kind of strange. You only need to beat a certain number of enemies.

Caldera Gate

❖ *Caldera Gate location*

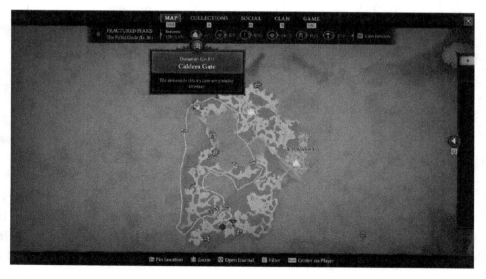

Caldera Gate is in the area of Fractured Peaks called Pallid Glade. This prison is west of the city of Menestad.

❖ Caldera Gate Dungeon

There are a lot of different monsters in Caldera Gate, and you'll have to watch out for the shamans. These monsters are easy to miss, and because of that, they can easily bring you down. Carver Overseers are also in this dungeon, so be ready to move out of the way when they swing their axes.

Fallen Idols need to be destroyed as the first goal of the dungeon. These idols are ground-based structures that shoot fireballs in two directions at once. These are also fast and have a slow cooldown, so you should expect to take a lot of damage from them. These idols are also guarded by a lot of enemies and elite monsters, so be careful when you attack them because you could easily lose all of your health in just one fight.

After you get rid of all the idols, you'll have to go to the next part of the dungeon. On the way there, there's a room that will trap you, and you'd have to pull the levers to get out. First, you have to destroy the ancient totems so you can get to the levers, and then you have to kill all the monsters.

The dungeon's second goal is to kill all of the monsters in the second area. This means you'll have to run around and look for opponents. Be careful not to get swarmed, because it can be hard to get through this dungeon's tight corridors if monsters are coming from both sides.

Since there is no boss in this dungeon, it's over once you've killed all of the enemies in the second area.

Cultist Refuge

❖ location of a Cult Refuge

The cathedral in Nostrava is where this prison is. The first city you reach is Nostrava, which is southwest of Kyovashad.

❖ Cultist Refuge Dungeon

This dungeon is full of cultists and werewolves who want to hurt you. like all dungeons, there will be a lot of monsters in here, and you will probably die if you get surrounded by them. So, keep an eye on your health at all times to avoid falling for this.

In the first area of the dungeon, the first goal is to kill all of the monsters.

You'll have to walk around to find them, but that shouldn't be a problem since the dungeon isn't that big and the enemies are just around the next corner. When you have killed all of them, an Overseer will drop down. The Overseer is an elite monster that you have to beat before you can move on to the next part of the dungeon.

On the way to the second part of the dungeon, there will be a room that locks itself, and you won't be able to leave until you destroy the structure in the middle. Get this done quickly and move on to the next area.

The high Priests need to be killed. This is the second goal in the dungeon. There are a few of these elite monsters in the second part of the dungeon. You'll have to walk around and look for them because this is a hunting quest Make sure you always look at your mini map for icons so you don't miss them.

Dead Man's Dredge

❖ *Where is Dead Man's Dredge?*

The Gale Valley area of the Fractured Peaks is where Dead Man's Dredge is. The dungeon is east of Yelesna, which is a town south of Kyovashad and to the east of Kyovashad.

❖ Dead Man's Dredge Dungeon

There are many different types of mobs in Dead Man's Dredge, from mages to sword fighters. Make sure you're ready, because this dungeon also has a lot of Ghouls who can easily surround you. In this dungeon, it will help you a lot to have crowd-control debuffs.

The dungeon's first goal is to get Animus from the carriers. Either Revenants or Blood Magi are behind these Carriers. You can find them on your minimap, so you'll need to move around the area and look for skulls on your minimap. They also call up a lot of monsters, so be ready for that as well.

The second goal is the same as the first. You'll still run around the second area, but now you'll be freeing prisoners. The prisoners are spread out all over the map, and a lot of monsters are keeping an eye on them.

Some of the prisoners are already dead, which can be confusing, but you still have to talk to them to lay them to rest because that's part of the goal. There is no boss in the dungeon, so once you set them all free (or buried them), the dungeon is done and you can get the reward.

Defiled Catacomb

❖ Where is the Defiled Catacomb?

The Defiled Catacomb is in the Desolate highlands in the Broken Peaks zone.

❖ Defiled Catacomb Dungeon

Spiders, Skeletons, and Skeletal Constructs are all enemies that live in the Defiled Catacomb. There are also a lot of spike traps, but they are easy to spot and easy to avoid. In the beginning of the dungeon, you have to kill a lot of monsters. When you try to destroy skeletal structures, that's when things get tricky.

In the second part of the dungeon, the Spiral Crypts, you can find Skeletal Constructs. As soon as you enter that zone, the goal changes to destroying the skeletal structures there. There are a lot of mobs guarding these structures, and some even have two elite mobs per structure.

The structure can also call up Bone Walls to protect itself from attacks, which can make it even harder to kill.

❖ Defiled Catacomb Dungeon Boss

The Broodguard is the boss of the Defiled Catacomb Dungeon. This boss isn't that dangerous cn its own. It shoots poison blobs that stay on the ground and poison anyone who steps on them, as well as webs that can trap your character.

But this boss's strength is that it can call up spider hosts that, when killed, will spawn a lot of spider eggs and hatchlings. When you add in the root and the poison blob, it can be very annoying.

Barbarians have a buff called "War Cry" that makes them unstoppable and makes them immune to the root when it is improved. It doesn't change the fact that there are a lot of other things that can easily kill you and swarm you

The best way to beat this boss is to move around a lot and make sure you don't get surrounded to begin with. Use your class's mobility, area-of-effect, or disabling abilities to stop the horde from getting to you. Then, when you've finished with them, go right to the boss.

Derelict lodge

❖ location of the Derelict lodge

Nostrava Deepwood is not too far away from Derelict lodge. It is west of Kyovashad and southwest of Menestad. It is north of Nevest.

❖ *Derelict lodge Dungeon*

Derelict lodge is a prison where bears and dead people walk around. The Bloated Corpsefiend is dangerous because it can just charge at you and blow up when it dies. You'll want to avoid the area-of-effect that happens when they die.

In the first part of this dungeon, you will walk around and check the bodies of dead villagers to see if they have the key to open the gate to the next area. To find these bodies, you'll have to walk around the dungeon for a long time. There's a pointer on the minimap that tells you if something is interesting or not.

If you find the key, you can open the gate to the next area. You will have to find and kill all of the Enforcers that are hiding in this part of the dungeon. Make sure you're ready to deal with these enforcers, who are surrounded by mobs and have been buffed. Once you've killed all of the enforcers, you'll be able to go into the boss room.

❖ Derelict lodge Boss

If you've already finished the lost Archives, you'll know this dungeon's boss. The Spiritcaller of Frost is the boss of Derelict lodge. The Spiritcaller of Frost calls forth totems all over the battlefield. When its projectile hits one of these totems, it bounces back, but this time with more projectiles. It can also use frost spells with a small area of effect (AoE) range.

You should try to avoid these spells because they can kill you when you have half health left. There will be a sound like what shamans use to tell their minions to come back to life. If you hear this, you should get going. Some monsters will also come to help the Spiritcaller.

One easy way to beat this boss is to face it away from the totems it made so that it can't multiply its projectiles. Aside from that, you'll be fighting it one-on-one most of the time as long as you get rid of the incoming mobs quickly. Also, you might want to have a skill that lets you get out of freeze because it can be pretty annoying.

Forbidden City

❖ Where is the Forbidden City?

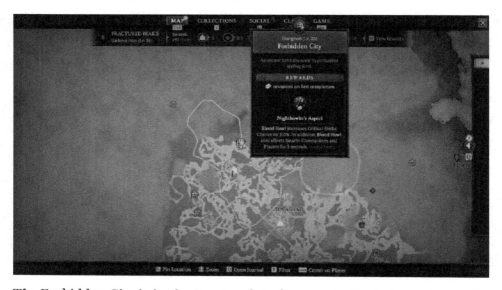

The Forbidden City is in the Fractured Peaks area, in the Sarkova Pass to be exact. It can be found north of Menestad.

❖ Forbidden City Dungeon

There are a lot of ghosts and wraiths in the Forbidden Dungeon. In fact, your very first goal will be to kill angry spirits. These spirits are hard to beat because they can summon lightning balls that hit pretty hard. Explore the dungeon and look for the angry ghosts to get to the next part of the dungeon.

The Ghastly Depths is the second part of the dungeon, and your job is to kill all the enemies there. This place is pretty big, so you'll be on your feet for a while. But this is just the beginning of the fun.

❖ Forbidden City Boss

Resurrected Malice is the name of the boss in this dungeon. If you're not used to dodging and you're a melee class, this boss can be very hard if it casts an AoE before sending out projectiles. The AoE will hurt you and push you back, and the projectiles will leave you open to attack, which can be very annoying over time.

The idea is that you can avoid getting hit by these or at least get hit less often if you run around the battlefield. The boss also sends out minions from time to time, but they aren't too hard to kill because they don't have that much health. Make sure to start with the fighter with a gun before you do anything else.

Forsaken Quarry

❖ location of the Forsaken Quarry

The Frigid Expanse area of the Fractured Peaks region is where the Forsaken Quarry is. The location of this dungeon is north of Kyovashad.

❖ Forsaken Quarry Dungeon

Ice Clan members are jumping around and throwing spears at you in the Forsaken Quarry. On top of that, there are walking corpses waiting for you. There are a lot of monsters in here with big axes that could easily stun or knock you down, so you'll want to make sure you use that dodge button.

The first goal in the dungeon is to clear the first area of enemies. There will be lots of mobs everywhere, so this one should be pretty easy to finish. Just wander around and kill every monster you see.

After that, it will be about setting prisoners free. The second part of the dungeon is full of prisoners. Some were dead, and some were still alive. Make sure you still talk to the dead prisoners to lay them to rest, as this is still part of the goal. If you missed one, look at your map or minimap to see if there is an icon of interest and go there.

One of the prisoners will have the key to open the next part of the dungeon. Once the gate is open, you can either kill all the monsters in the next area or go straight to the dungeon boss.

❖ Forsaken Quarry Boss

The Khazra Abomination is in charge of Forsaken Quarry. This boss doesn't have any followers, so it will just be you and it. Its main move is to throw poisonous AoEs that stay on the ground for a long time. This means that the boss fight will require a lot of moving around.

The boss monster doesn't have any other tricks. You should be fine as long as you don't stay in those AoEs.

hallowed Ossuary

❖ Place of the hallowed Ossuary

The hallowed Ossuary is in the area of the Fractured Peaks called the Frigid Expanse. This cave is located east of Kyovashad.

❖ hallowed Ossuary Dungeon

There are maggots, corpses on the move, and blood mages everywhere in hallowed Ossuary. There are also some revenants, so be aware that they can lunge at you and be ready to avoid them. There are a lot of plague maggots in here, and when they work together, they can do a lot of damage. But if they're just by themselves, they're not that much of a problem.

The first goal of this dungeon is to get Animus from people carrying Animus These carriers are elite monsters, and "Animus Carrier" will be written next to their names. You can also find them on your minimap, so make sure to check it often so you don't miss one.

Once you have all of the Anima you need, you'll have to find the urn and put them in it. After that, the door to the next level will open.

Your next goal is to find the bloodstone and put it back on the pedestal. To find it, you'll have to do a lot of walking, but if you're lucky and have taken the right turns, you might find it right away. There are a lot of mobs, including elite enemies, guarding these bloodstones, so keep an eye on your health at all times.

When you put it back on the pedestal, the door to the boss room will open.

❖ hallowed Ossuary Boss

The Blood Bishop is the boss of the hallowed Ossuary. This boss has been in different dungeons, like the Immortal Emanation. The key to beating this boss is to avoid getting hit by its powerful attacks, like the violet fog projectile, the command grab, and the flesh it creates.

The command grab is easy to get away from if you move around and use the dodge button. The flesh boils and projectiles are the hardest to avoid. For the projectiles, it's best to keep your distance and start moving around as soon as you see a violet fog in front of the Blood Bishop.

The bishop calls this thing after it burrows its tentacles into the ground, which makes the flesh boil. Try to destroy as much flesh as you can before it explodes, because it does AoE damage that can kill you if you let it.

hoarfrost Demise

❖ *how to look for hoarfrost Demise*

In Fractured Peaks, hoarfrost Demise is on the northwest side of the Seat of the heavens.

❖ *hoarfrost Demise*

Follow the main path once you're in the dungeon, and you'll meet some enemies right away that you'll have to kill. When you get to the first open room, you should turn right.

This will take you to a room with two ways out. After you've taken care of the enemies, go back to the right path. When you get to the fork, turn right again

As soon as you get to the bottom, you'll find the first Skeletal Construct you need to destroy. As soon as you start attacking it, enemies will start to appear, so be ready to fight.

Now that you've destroyed the first building, keep walking back until you reach the intersection you were at before. This time, turn left when you get there. This will lead you to a four-way path. When that happens, turn left and go down the hall.

This will take you to the second Skeletal Construct. Just like the other, once you hit it, you should be ready for a fight.

After you destroy the second structure, go back to the four-way intersection and turn left. This will take you to the last building.

After that, you will need to go back to the four-way path and turn right. This will lead you to a healing Well near another hallway.

As soon as you walk down the hall and into the next room, the boss fight will begin.

❖ *hoarfrost Demise Boss*

The Khazra Abomination will be there when you walk into the room. This boss likes to get close to you and fight, but it can also throw acid at you. During the whole fight, it will alternate between hitting the ground, throwing acid at you, and surrounding the area with acid. You won't have too much trouble fighting it if your character is good at long range, but if your character is good at close combat, you should hit and run.

❖ *hoarfrost Demise Rewards*

When you beat the boss, you'll get the Blood-bathed Aspect as a reward.

Immortal Emanation

❖ *location of Immortal Emanation*

Immortal Emanation is in the area of Fractured Peaks called Frigid Expanse which is east of Kyovashad.

❖ *Immortal Emanation Dungeon*

Immortal Emanation is full of ghouls, and they will usually mob you, so make sure you always have a lot of hP or are very aware of how much you have. Aside from that, these are normal monsters, so standard tactics like killing the ones with ranged attacks and so on will work.

The first thing you have to do in the dungeon is get rid of the blood boils. Blood boils look like large red bumps on the ground. They do look a little bit more horrifying, which is a typical Diablo move. Anyway, a lot of monsters keep coming and protecting these blood boils. Not only that, but they also make smaller boils called flesh that explode after a while.

Because of this, you might want to start by getting rid of the flesh before going after the boils.

When you've killed all of the blood boils, you'll be told to move on to the next area. But there will be a room with spikes and two levers on the way there. There will also be a lot of mobs in here, but you can quickly get rid of most of them by using the spikes.

After you've killed everything and pulled the lever, you can move on. Now, you can either kill all the monsters in this room or go straight to the boss room.

❖ Immortal Emanation Boss

The Blood Bishop is the boss of this dungeon. The Blood Bishop has a few dangerous moves, but the most dangerous ones are the tentacles that summon flesh (like the blood boils) and the violet fog that shoots a lot of projectiles.

here, you should try to destroy as much flesh as you can because these things can kill you. Then, when you see a purple fog in front of the Blood Bishop, get ready to move around and dodge. This boss also has a command grab that can be broken by going unstoppable or dodging at the right time. If he grabs you, he will take your life force.

Kor Dragan Barracks

❖ location of the Kor Dragan Barracks

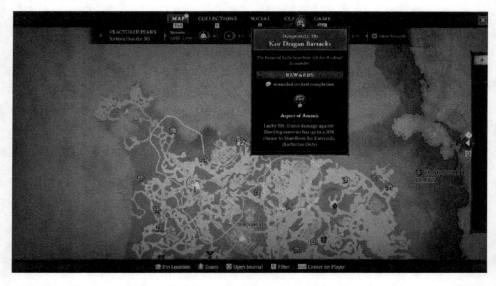

The Kor Dragan Stronghold is close to the Kor Dragan Barracks. This stronghold is in the Kor Dragan area of the Fractured Peaks and is directly north of Kyovashad on the world map. This place is also east of Menestad.

❖ Kor Dragan Barracks

The Kor Dragan Barracks is a big dungeon with a lot of monsters. The goals in this dungeon also take advantage of this by making you look for different things all over the place.

The gate control devices in the first area of the dungeon are the first thing on the list. These devices look like levers with chains on them. You can either run around looking for these devices or take out the mobs one at a time.

After you turn them all on, you'll have to move on to the next part of the dungeon. But on the way, you'll run into a room where you'll be trapped and have to fight mobs. Just kill these enemies, and you can go to the next area.

The second thing you have to do in the dungeons is look for blood boils. These look a lot like the ones in Kor Dragan, and like them, they can call on flesh to protect themselves. Try to kill the flesh boils first so they don't do damage to an area around them.

Since there is no boss in this dungeon, when you kill all of the boils, the dungeon will be done.

light's Watch

❖ Where is light's Watch?

light's Watch is in Fractured Peaks, southeast of Kyovashad and northeast of Nevesk. At the east gate of Kyovashad, there is a small road that leads there.

❖ light's Watch location

There are a lot of enemies in this dungeon that will deal AoE damage and DoT, which can be very annoying. There will be a lot of enemies, just like in other dungeons. The first thing you have to do in the dungeon is find and kill the Watchmen. These enemies will have the key to the next part of the dungeon.

There are more of the same kinds of enemies in the second part of the dungeon as there were in the first. Make sure to avoid their ground-based DoTs and AoE damage as much as possible. The Firebrand is a monster to watch out for. One of its moves is to slam its mace on the ground, which will knock you down if it hits you. Use your dodge to get away from this move.

As you go deeper, you will meet Revenants and Blood Magi.

❖ light's Watch Dungeon

The boss of the light's Watch is called the Den Mother. At first, she might not look like she's doing much damage, but she has a move where she stomps on the ground and makes AoEs appear. Over time, stepping on these will hurt you.

After a while, these little AoEs will go away. The Den Mother can also call up packs of wolves that will knock you down if they attack you. So, if you see one getting ready, you might want to dodge it or use a buff that makes you impossible to stop.

lost Archives

❖ lost Archives location

Southwest of Nevesk is where lost Archives is located. It's an abandoned library full of monsters with abilities that make it hard to move.

❖ lost Archives Dungeon

lost Archives is a pretty boring dungeon because not only do debuffs fly around that slow or stop your movement, but you also have to look for these two mechanical boxes to trigger the boss fight.

This makes everything much more boring than it already is, and it can be hard on classes that can't deal with mobs and have trouble with debuffs that slow their movement. Since this dungeon is pretty big, the best way to deal with it is to just take your time and not be in a hurry.

There are also monsters that explode when they touch you. So you need to be ready to move out of their area of effect.

❖ *lost Archives Boss*

The boss of the lost Archives is called the Spiritcaller of Frost, and it does exactly what you think it does: it shoots ice projectiles that can slow you down and calls on monsters that will kill you. Even though it isn't that strong by itself, its hP can be quite a problem.

It also calls up pillars that, if hit, increase the number of projectiles it fires. So, you should move away from it so that dodging these projectiles is easier. Also, if you let the summons pile up, they can get pretty annoying. Managing the mobs is easier if you can stun or root them. You could also just kill everything, and that would also work.

Maulwood

❖ Where is Maulwood?

East of Margrave is where Maulwood is. Margrave is between Kyovashad and Nevesk. It is southeast of Kyovashad and northeast of Nevesk.

❖ Maulwood Dungeon

There are a lot of Wood Wraiths in Maulwood. Because they are so big and strong, they can be very annoying. With their attacks, they can also move you or stun you for a short time. The Firebrand is also here with his trusty mace, which can knock you down.

In the first part of the dungeon, you have to run around the area and kill bandit sentries. These sentries have been buffed and can be dangerous to players who don't see them coming. Most of the time, it will stop you by making you scared or frozen, so keep an eye on it at all times.

After this, you'll find the entrance to the second area and be told to destroy structures made of bones. This time, there are no bone walls that will stop you from getting close, but a lot of monsters will attack you at once, so keep an eye on your hP.

This dungeon doesn't have a boss, which might seem good at first, but once you get to the skeletal structure part, there are so many mobs that it can be hard to keep up. If your character can't do much to deal with mobs, make sure to kite around. It will be easier for characters to get through this dungeon if they can handle them well.

Mercy's Reach

❖ *Where is Mercy's Reach?*

Mercy's Reach is in the area of Fractured Peaks, in Sarkova Pass. This is on the way to Scosglen on one of the roads that connect to it. The dungeon is north of Kyovashad and to the northwest.

❖ *Mercy's Reach Dungeon*

In the first area of Mercy's Reach, there are a lot of Quillrats. Because of their range and damage, these monsters can be very annoying when there are a lot of them. Also, they will kite you around, which means that if you're a melee fighter, you'll have to chase them around.

The first goal of the dungeon is to find the Knight hunters and kill them. These elite monsters are knight hunters, and they have different buffs on them. Since this is just a killing quest, you can just kill the targets and move on to the next area without killing any other mobs.

When you get to the next area, the goal changes to a fetch quest. This time, you'll look for boxes with moving parts. You can only carry one, so you'll have to go get them one by one and put them back on the pedestal.

Putting them in the pedestal will open the door, and along the way you'll come to a room with four totems and a lot of monsters. First, take care of the totems, then deal with the monsters.

Once that's done, you don't really need to kill any more monsters. You can just ignore them and go straight to the room with the boss.

❖ *Mercy's Reach Boss*

The Tomb lord is in charge of Mercy's Reach. The Tomb lord can move around and make you lose your sight. It can also use Bone Wall to make the bones explode in an area of effect. So, if your hP is low, you should stay away from the bone walls it makes because they do a lot of damage.

Skeletons will also appear from time to time, so you may want to deal with them quickly. The blind AoE it drops is also a DoT that will drain your life as long as you are in the AoE. The key is to avoid the area-of-effect attacks that the Tomb lord is dropping.

Nostrava Deepwood

❖ *Where is Nostrava Deepwood?*

Nostrava Deepwood is in the area of Fractured Peaks called Pallid Glade. It is right north of Nevesk and west of Kyovashad.

❖ *Nostrava Deepwood Dungeon*

Nostrava is a dungeon where lots and lots of mobs are moving around. There are skeletons, skeleton structures, wood wraiths, and even quillrats. All of these are kind of annoying, and some of them can even slow you down.

In the first part of the dungeon, you'll have to kill every enemy in the first area. Since the place is pretty big, this can take a lot of time. Then you'll have to find the entrance to the second area, where a skeleton-like structure is waiting.

Do this quickly, because a lot of mobs will spawn as you get close to the building. Use the barrels around you to get rid of the mobs. After you break down the building, the next step is to kill Treebones. There are a lot of mobs around these enemies, which have been buffed and beefed up. look for a skull on the minimap to find them.

Three of these guys are going to be in the area. Worse news? This dungeon is pretty big, so you'll spend most of your time just looking for them and walking around. Because of this, you might want to use skills that make you move faster if you want to get around the area quickly.

Rimescar Cavern

❖ *Where is Rimescar Cavern?*

The Rimescar Cavern is in the town of Malnok. Malnok is east of Kyovashad. The Bear Tribe Refuge, which is north of Malnok, is also close by.

❖ *Rimescar Cavern Dungeon*

There are a lot of ice clansmen in Rimescar Cavern, which would usually make it hard to move around. So, to get out of these slows and freezes, you would need something that makes you impossible to stop.

The first thing you have to do in the dungeon is find and kill the sacrificial flesh. Even though the dungeon isn't that big, the halls are long and narrow. Make sure you won't be surrounded by enemies when you get close to the sacrificial flesh. These structures are guarded by a lot of enemies.

Once all of the sacrificial flesh has been destroyed, the next step is to go to the next dungeon. On the way, a room will lock you in and let out a lot of monsters and elite monsters. here, the goal is just to stay alive while the enemies attack, so deal with them however you want.

Go to the second room after that. The next thing you need to do is break through the Ice Barrier that is blocking the way to the boss room. When you find it, just do that, and get ready for a boss fight.

❖ Rimescar Cavern Boss

The Khazra Abomination is in charge of Rimescar Cave. This dungeon boss does most of its damage to you with AoEs that stay on the ground, so if you can kite it, make sure to take full advantage of that.

The Khazra Abomination will always try to follow you, so if you try to run away, it will do a charge move and walk towards you while shooting you with its area-of-effect attacks that deal damage over time and slow you down. For this fight, all you have to do is make sure you don't step on the AoEs and keep doing damage.

Sanguine Chapel

❖ Sanguine Chapel location

The Sanguine Chapel is in the subregion of Fractured Peaks called Seat of heavens. This part of the world is east of Kyovashad.

❖ Sanguine Chapel Dungeon

This dungeon is pretty big, and the first task will use that to your advantage. The first goal of the dungeon is to find the mechanical boxes and put them back on the pedestals where they belong. Since the dungeon is pretty big, you'll spend a lot of time just walking around looking for them. These boxes are also guarded by a lot of mobs, including elite ones. As a side note, you can only pick up one box at a time.

When you put them on their pedestals, the door to the next area opens and you can go there. When you get to the next area, your next goal will be to kill all of the monsters in that area. Just walk around and kill everything you see.

The dungeon boss comes after you've killed everything in your way.

❖ *Sanguine Chapel Boss*

The Blood Bishop is the top boss of the dungeon. Pretty good, huh? There are three things you need to worry about with this boss. Projectiles made of flesh, grab, and violet fog. You can see the violet fog projectiles in front of the Blood Bishop, so if you see them, stop fighting right away.

When the Blood Bishop burrows its tentacles into the ground, boils of flesh appear on the ground. After a certain amount of time, these boils will pop and deal AoE damage. So, you should try to destroy as much of their flesh as you can before they explode, since they can easily take away a lot of your hP.

last, there is the command grab. Even though this attack is easy to avoid, it is still dangerous. If it gets you, the Blood Bishop will drink your blood to heal itself.

Tormented Ruins

❖ *Where is Tormented Ruins?*

North of Nevesk is where you can find the Tormented Ruins.

❖ *Tormented Ruins Dungeon*

Tormented Ruins doesn't have a lot of mechanics. It's mostly just a normal Diablo dungeon where you can go in and beat up demons and skeletons. Some enemies can freeze you, but that's pretty much it. Try to kill these monsters, which usually have ranged attacks, first so that you can move around the battlefield freely.

having an ability to control a crowd is also helpful in this dungeon and in general when you're surrounded by a mob. Stun them, and then give them hell. Some of the enemies here can also throw up obstacles that force you to fight them one-on-one, so you should kill those enemies first before moving on to the next part of the dungeon.

❖ Tormented Ruins Boss

The Scourge of the land is the boss of the Tormented Ruins. he uses a big weapon that hits the ground and causes a small area of effect. The Scourge of the land can use these small AoEs as portals to summon demons that will help him destroy you.

These portals disappear after a long time, so you can't just sit around and wait for them to go away. The best way to deal with it is to kill the spawns and then kill the boss.

When it comes to the boss himself, he uses his weapon in a mix of attacks and swings. Watch out for his fire breath and when he slams his weapon.

Zenith

❖ Where is Zenith?

Zenith is in the northeastern part of Fractured Peaks, close to where the name is written on the map of the world. It is northeast of Kyovashad.

❖ Zenith Dungeon

Monsters like skeletons, revenants, and blood magi live in Zenith. Because the corridors in this dungeon are pretty small, these enemies can be pretty annoying, especially if they have AoE attacks. You'll be pressing that button a lot in here, so get ready to dodge.

The first goal in the dungeon is to find and kill the guards who have been brought back to life. So, you're going to have to run all over the dungeon to find them. After that, you'll face a skeleton-like structure that you'll have to beat. There will be a lot of mobs, and the skeletal structure will sometimes call up bone walls around it.

The next step would be to find bloodstones and put them back on the pedestals. So, yes, you will explore the second part of the dungeon. Worse, you can't pick them all up at once and put them back on the pedestals; you have to do it one by one. Pick one up, put it on a pedestal, and then look for the next one.

Once you have all the bloodstones, you can turn on the statue of ice to reveal the boss.

❖ *Zenith Boss*

The Blood Bishop is the boss of Zenith. You'll have to be careful with this boss because it has abilities that can knock you out. The first thing to notice is that it shoots violet projectiles. At first, this will look like a purple fog. When you see that, you should run away and try to stay out of the way of the projectiles that will follow.

The next thing to remember is the fleshes it calls forth. After the Blood Bishop moves its tentacles, these fleshes will appear. When you see this, you need to kill as many of them as you can because they do a lot of AoE damage that can kill you.

Zenith also has a command grab that will take your health and use it to heal itself if it hits you. Try not to do this. If you can't be stopped, then this move won't work.

Ancient's lament

❖ *Ancient's lament location*

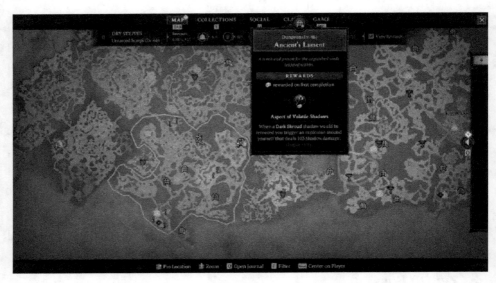

Ancient's lament is in the part of Dry Steppes called Untamed Scarps. This area is south of Ked Bardu and includes the small town of Jirandai.

❖ *Ancient's lament Dungeon*

There is no boss in this dungeon. But there are a lot of enemies there who probably won't leave you alone until you kill them all. As was already said, the hallways in this dungeon are very narrow. This means you'll want to make sure you don't get crowded, so bring skills that help you control crowds or deal with the monsters in front of you right away to reduce the chance of getting mobbed.

The first thing you have to do in this dungeon is find ancient statues and put them back on their bases. like other quests like this one, you can only pick up one of them. As soon as you start to grab one, the other one falls down. These statues are guarded by both normal and elite monsters, so you should be ready to fight a lot of enemies before you get one.

Once you put them back on the pedestal, you can move on to the next area.

If you go through the door, you'll end up in a locked room where you'll have to fight off waves of enemies before the doors can be opened. Before you go in, make sure your health is full and your skills are ready. Once you're done with this, your next goal is to find Demonic Corruptions.

These structures, which are called "Elite Monsters," are called "Demonic Corruptions." They are also protected by large groups of monsters and elite monsters. Just destroy these structures, and the dungeon should be over.

Bloodsoaked Crag

❖ *Where is Bloodsoaked Crag?*

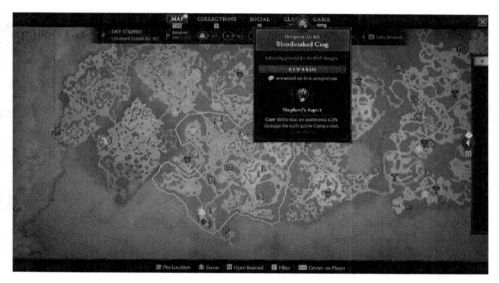

Bloodsoaked Crag is in the part of Dry Steppes called Untamed Scarps. There are several dungeons and Jirandai in this area.

❖ *Bloadsoaked Crag Dungeon*

This dungeon is pretty big, and there are a lot of ways to get from one area to another. Not only that, but the sheer number of mobs in this area can be overwhelming if you don't know how to handle a crowd. Because of this, you should make sure to have one. Be careful around here because the big monsters, like the Flesh Mauler, can stun you. When you see them both raise their weapons, be ready to dodge at the right time.

The first goal of the dungeon is to look around the first area for prisoners.

Some of these prisoners are dead, just like in other quests where you have to free prisoners. But you still have to talk to them in order to put them to rest. Part of the goal is still to do this. As soon as you set them free, two elite monsters will appear. Take care of the two of them so you can move on to the next area.

The second area seems bigger than the first one because you can move between camps by doing things like hanging from a tight rope and so on. In the second area, the goal is to kill Animus Carriers and steal their Animus. The Animus are the purple fogs that they leave behind when they die, so be sure to pick these up.

When you have enough, find the urn to put them in and do something with it. The seal will open, letting you into the room where the boss is.

❖ Bloodsoaked Crag Boss

The Chief Marauder is the boss of Bloodsoaked Crag. This boss wants to keep things close and personal. There are only about two moves that you really need to know. The first one is an attack that is like a Barbarian's jump. Usually, he does this after a warcry that makes you move away from him.

The second is a ground slam, which sends a wind projectile in both directions when it hits the ground. To avoid these two moves, just stand behind him or dodge to get behind him before he uses them.

Carrion Fields

❖ Where is Carrion Fields?

The Scarred Coast area of Dry Steppes is where Carrion Fields is. The southwest corner of Ked Bardu is where this dungeon is.

❖ Carrion Fields Dungeon

The only really annoying thing about this dungeon is how big it is. Combine this with the fact that your first goal is to find the Ancients Statues and put them back on their pedestals. When you're looking for it, you'll see how big the dungeon really is.

This can be a problem for characters who have trouble getting rid of a lot of mobs quickly. If you aren't careful, they can easily overwhelm you. But you shouldn't have any problems because this is the only thing you have to do in this dungeon before you can get to the boss.

like other fetch quests in dungeons, you can only move one at a time. This means you'll have to pick one up, put it on the pedestal, look for another one and then do the same thing again.

There are also plants and traps in this area that can slow you down or hurt you, so pay attention to where you are.

❖ Carrion Fields Boss

The Tomb lord is the boss of Carrion Fields. When fighting this boss, you need to be perfectly positioned, so pay attention to where you are standing. When fighting the Tomb lord, you need to be aware of two things.

The first is the blind area of effect that it drops. You won't be able to cast spells while you're in it, and you'll go blind. Not only that, but it does a lot of damage over time as well. Just stay away from these as much as possible.

The second one is the bone walls that it calls up. The Tomb lord has a power that can make these walls explode, so if you see blue smoke coming from the walls, make sure to run away so you don't get hit. If the player isn't in the right place when the Tomb lord uses this move, the run can be over.

Champion's Demise

❖ Place of Champion's Death

Champion's Demise is in the part of Dry Steppes called Untamed Scarps. This part of the world is south of Ked Bardu and close to Jirandai.

❖ Champion's Demise Dungeon

Champions' Demise is a pretty big dungeon, and it will make sure to take advantage of that. Because of this, there will be a lot of monsters wandering around in big groups.

The first goal of the dungeon is to find stone carvings and put them back on their stands. Because the dungeon is so big, you'll have to spend some time walking around. Monsters guard these stone carvings, which are found in small camps.

like similar quests, you can only bring one of these with you at a time. This will add even more time to the time it takes to reach this goal.

When you have put all of them on the pedestals, two elite monsters will appear. You have to beat these two before you can move on in the dungeon.

❖ **Champion's Demise Boss**

The Khazra Abomination is the boss of Champion's Demise. This boss wants to fight you face-to-face, which is good for melee jobs. When fighting this boss, there is really only one thing to watch out for, and that is the AoE it makes.

This boss throws an AoE that stays on the ground. If you step on it, it will hurt you, so it's best to move around every so often so you can stay away from it. It also has a move that charges at you if you are too far away.

Charnel house

❖ **Where is Charnel house?**

This dungeon is in the part of the Dry Steppes called Untamed Scarps. This place is close to Jirandai, which is south of Ked Bardu.

❖ **Charnel house Dungeon**

Some dungeons are bigger than this one. It stays about the same size, which helps with the first goal in the dungeon, which is to get the prisoners out. These prisoners are in cages, and this whole dungeon is a prison, so there will be a lot of doors to open, which can make rooms feel very small at times.

So, it might be best to chase the enemies around until you find a place that isn't too crowded. The Gorger is an enemy you should watch out for. This enemy can put you to sleep with its weapons. So, you'll want to keep an eye on that monster at all times. When it raises both hands, you'll want to get out of the way.

When you're done freeing the prisoners, you'll fight a mini-boss. This mini-boss is guarding the key to the next area, which you need to get to.

This mini-boss is probably one of the most annoying you'll face, so it could be the dungeon boss. It can charge at you, throw poison AoEs that slow and damage you, and use a structure it summons to root you.

Because of this, you'll want to focus on destroying the "hellbinder," which is the structure it summons to root you, so that you can safely kite around or change positions when there are a lot of poison AoEs around you.

After beating the boss, get the key to the next area and go there. In this second area, you'll have to find the corpse piles and destroy them. These piles also send out poisons that have an area of effect and stay on the ground for a while before going away.

When all the corpse piles have been completely destroyed, the dungeon is done.

Komdor Temple

❖ *Where is the Komdor Temple?*

The Scarred Coast part of the Dry Steppes is where the Komdor Temple is. The southwest corner of Ked Bardu is where this dungeon is.

❖ *Komdor Temple Dungeon*

We've already said that this dungeon is full of Goatmen. The first thing you need to do in the dungeon is find the high priests and kill them. This can take a lot of time because the place is so big and full of different kinds of monsters, including elite ones.

Most of the time, you'll find high Priests at the edge of the map. They usually have a couple of elite monsters with them, which can be hard to deal with if you're not paying attention to your hP that much.

You can also try to get through the dungeon quickly by ignoring the monsters and just looking for the high Priests. But remember that some of these will follow you to the end of the dungeon, so be ready to deal with them even then.

After you kill all of the high Priests, you can open the door to the chamber and face the dungeon boss.

❖ Komdor Temple Boss

The Khazra Abomination is the boss of the Komdor Temple. This boss wants to fight you face-to-face, which is good for melee jobs. When fighting this boss, there is really only one thing to watch out for, and that is the AoE it makes.

This boss throws an AoE that stays on the ground. If you step on it, it will hurt you, so it's best to move around every so often so you can stay away from it. It also has a move that charges at you if you are too far away.

Path of the Blind

❖ Where is Path of the Blind?

Path of the Blind is in the area of Dry Steppes called Khargai Crags. East of Ked Bardu is where the dungeon is.

❖ Path of the Blind Dungeon

As was already said, this dungeon is full of monsters that can kill you if you're not careful. Since your first goal is to kill the Blind Guardians, there is a good chance that this will happen. These guardians can shoot big fireballs all around them, and they are also surrounded by enemies.

With that in mind, you should always be aware of what you're stepping on and how much hP you have.

The second goal is to find the Bloodstones that are hidden around the area.

This area is a temple, and it's pretty big. Because of this, you'll spend quite a bit of time walking around and looking for bloodstones. You can only take them one at a time, so you'll have to go back to the pedestal a lot for this one When all of the bloodstones are on the pedestal, the boss of the dungeon will show up.

❖ *Path of the Blind Boss*

The Scourge of the land is the boss of the Path of the Blind Dungeon. This boss has a mace that it uses to hit you and hit the ground to make an area of effect that lasts for a long time. Walking on these will hurt you in the long run, so you should move out of the way.

These AoEs also let the boss call demons to fight for him through portals. To beat this boss, make sure you don't get hit by its powerful moves, such as the triple slam, and don't step on the AoEs.

Sealed Archives

❖ *Sealed Archives location*

This dungeon is in the part of the Dry Steppes called Untamed Scarps. This place is close to Jirandai, which is south of Ked Bardu.

❖ *Sealed Archives Dungeon*

Sealed Archives is a dungeon that is pretty big. It looks a lot like the lost Archives dungeon in the Fractured Peaks, where it is also located. You will also spend a lot of time walking around, which is similar to what you did before.

The first thing you need to do in the dungeon is find the Decayed Keymaster and kill it. This is an elite monster that has the key you need to get to the next part of the dungeon. When fighting this monster, you need to be careful because it is surrounded by a large group of monsters that can make it hard to beat. Keep an eye on your map and minimap at all times. A skull icon will appear to show where it is.

Use the key to open the door once you've defeated the Keymaster. After you open the door, you'll find yourself in a room full of traps and monsters. Do what you want with them and move on to the next area.

The second area is kind of like the first one, but this time you have to kill everything in it. So just go around destroying everything you see. After that, it's time for the boss to come.

❖ Sealed Archives Boss

The Tomb lord is the boss of the Sealed Archives. This boss monster is pretty weak, so as long as you move carefully, you should be able to beat it. When you fight the Tomb lord, there are two things you need to remember.

First, it has AoE that blinds. If you stand on this AoE for too long, it will hurt you. So it's best to stay away from them. The second is that it calls up bone walls. This one can be tricky because the Tomb lord can make these walls blow up. You will take a lot of damage if you aren't careful and are close to the wall. If you're surrounded by them, use a skill that lets you move somewhere far away from them. You could also just break down the walls.

Seaside Descent

❖ location of Seaside Descent

Seaside Descent is in a part of Dry Steppes called Kotama Grasslands. West of Ked Bardu is where this dungeon is.

❖ Seaside Descent Dungeon

As was already said, there is no boss in this dungeon. You will have to walk around a lot and look for monsters, though, because the first goal of the dungeon is to kill all of the monsters in the first area.

Now, this might have been easy, but the number of skeleton archers and corpse bows can make it hard for melee classes, who will have to walk around chasing them. The fact that the monsters in this area are sometimes spread out doesn't help either.

When you get to the second area of the dungeon, your second goal is to look for piles of dead bodies and destroy them. There are a lot of monsters and some elites guarding these piles of dead bodies.

HOW TO GUIDES

CRAFTING, MATERIALS, AND COLLECTIBLES

How to Increase Potion Capacity & Efficiency

❖ *How to Carry More Potions*

The more healing potions a player has, the more times they can use them when they are hurt. No matter how good you are at Diablo, that is one of the most important parts of the game. But it's important to remember that players can't stock up on potions to get ready for a tough fight, and there are only so many to go around, at least at the beginning of the game.

The most healing potions a player can start with are four, but they can get more by picking up drops from dead enemies or chests. This can only be increased by using all of Diablo 4's features and, more importantly, by earning Renown.

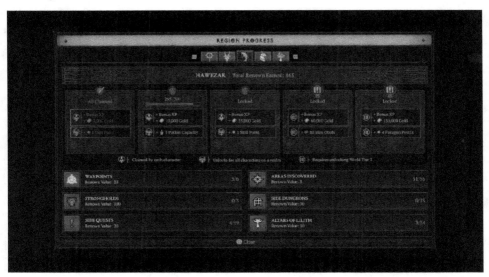

In the game, there are five different regions where players can do different things to earn Renown. One way is to find Altars of Lilith. Another is to clear out dungeons, which always pay a good amount of the currency.

And when a player has 300 Renown, they can get the second reward for making progress in a region. This reward gives them +1 Potion Capacity, plus extra XP and Gold. This is true for all of the regions, so players can use up to nine potions by the end.

❖ *How to Improve Healing Efficiency*

Even with that many potions, end-game players need a lot more healing than people who are just starting out. This is because enemies deal more damage and have more health. If you want to know what's going on, you should stop by the Herbalist every now and then.

They let players trade things they find in the wild, like Gallowvine and Biteberry, to make healing potions even better. At level 10, 15, 20, and so on you can do this. Even though resources are always easy to find in the world, the hardest part for players will be meeting the requirements for higher levels.

Once this is done, potions will be more useful than ever, letting all classes fight longer and harder to stop the terrible things that are now attacking Sanctuary.

Whispers of the Dead Explained

❖ *What are Whispers of the Dead in Diablo 4?*

Those who have played through the main storyline of Diablo 4 will recognise the name of this part of the game. It has everything to do with the Tree of Whispers in Hawezar.

After Elias was killed and his head brought back to the Tree as payment, the dead Horadrim are still a constant annoyance because they are now one of many talking heads on the Tree. After you finish the main story, you can go back to the Tree to find something new to do.

If you agree to what the Tree of Whispers wants, new icons will show up on the map to show active Whispers that are only available for a limited time. This can be as simple as killing a certain number of enemies or as hard as clearing out dungeons and cellars.

❖ Whispers of the Dead Rewards

Depending on the type of Whisper, players will get a certain number of Grim Favours when they finish it. For every 10 Grim Favours they get, they can go back to the Tree of Whispers and get valuable rewards.

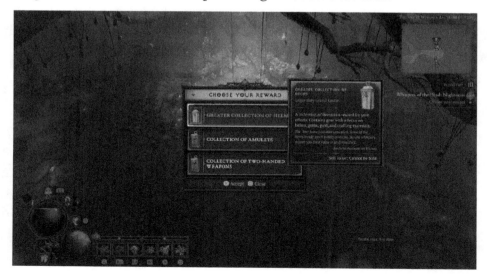

Talk to the Tree of Whispers when you have at least 10 Grim Favours with you, and it will give you three choices for a reward. Each option is clearly made for a certain equipment slot and comes with gems, gold, crafting materials, and a big XP boost. Whispers of the Dead is a great end-game activity because you can sometimes find Legendary Grand Caches and other types of caches that give even stronger gear.

Diablo 4's path to the level cap is long and hard, so you need all the help you can get to keep the monsters at bay and look good while doing it. End-game players need to get more cool stuff through Whispers of the Dead to keep going.

How to Get Whispering Keys

❖ Where to Buy Whispering Keys

In Diablo 4, Purveyor of Curiosities vendors are the only ones who sell Whispering Keys. In Diablo 4, there are eight of these shops. They are in almost every major city. Here's what they are:

- Kyovashad: The NPC's name is Lizveth, and you can find her by looking southeast of the fast travel Waypoint.

- Yelesna, the NPC is called Rodyar, and you can find him near the Inn.

- Near the Backwater Waypoint, on Exile's Heap

- Zarbinzet: Near the door to the south.

- Gea Kul: Along the wall to the north.

- Jirandai Waypoint: To find this, go south. Purveyor

- Ked Bardu: From the Waypoint, go north until the players are near the town's outer wall.

- A little to the south of the Waypoint, says Cerrigar.

Whispering Keys can be bought from these vendors for 20 Murmuring Obols. Murmuring Obols are a special currency that can be found in chests, dungeons, and as a reward for beating the World Boss Ashava in World Events.

❖ Are Whispering Keys Worth It in Diablo 4?

Silent Chests can appear almost anywhere in Diablo 4, but they only show up on a player's minimap for a short time. At the time this was written, it didn't seem like Silent Chests appeared in any kind of order. It also didn't seem like the items inside were chosen at random. This makes it hard to say for sure whether or not the Whispering Keys are worth the 20 Murmuring Obols they cost.

Most likely, early in the game, players would be better off spending their Obols on other things in the Purveyor of Curiosities. Players can choose an item type they know they can use, like a cap, a two-handed axe, a wand, or an amulet. They will get a common to legendary item of that type with a random set of stats.

So, instead of relying on whatever the Silent Chest gives them, players are sure to get an item they know will be useful. But the chests can hold a lot of Diablo 4 gold, which some players might want more than items.

How to Farm Fiend Rose

❖ What are Diablo 4's Fiend Roses?

As part of the end-game grind in Diablo 4, players will need to be able to change the affixes on their weapons, armour, and other gear. Through the Enchant Item system, players can swap out an item's affix if it's almost perfect but has one that's not useful. To enchant an item, they will need the item and one Fiend Rose, which will be used to choose the affix to change.

This rare plant can be found in a few places, but which is the best? Now that Diablo 4 is out, they might want to know how to get the most Fiend Roses from their farms.

❖ Where to Find Fiend Roses

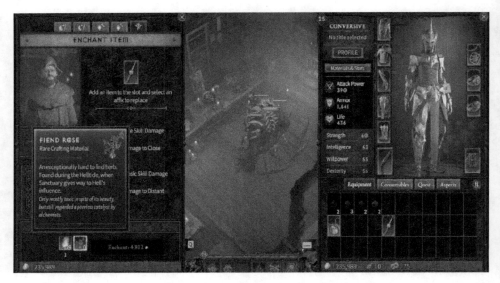

Fiend Roses can be found in chests and when fighting strong PvE enemies, but the best place to farm them is during Helltide events. Helltides won't happen in Diablo 4 until a player has reached World Tier Level 3, which means they are at least level 50.

These end-game events that change the environment will change the whole landscape of Sanctuary, giving players access to more difficult enemies and different kinds of collectibles and money. Not only will the landscape look different and be much more dangerous, but Helltide will also change the plants, which will let the poisonous Fiend Roses grow. These rare Roses will grow in the hellish terrain of Helltides and can be farmed like any other plant in Diablo 4.

But if they're lucky, they might find one or two Fiend Roses by accident. You can sometimes find these roses in Silent Chests that you can only open with Whispering Keys. They can also sometimes drop from bosses in dungeons or in the world. The more difficult a battle is, the more likely it is that a random Fiend Rose will drop. This chance goes up as a player's world level goes up.

Abstruse Sigil - Where to Get and How to Use

❖ *How to Get Abstruse Sigil*

When it comes to this material, players will have to be patient because it's not easy to get, and it can take a while to get even a small number of them. To get an Abstruse Sigil, players must take Legendary jewellery to a blacksmith and have it repaired. Rings and Amulets are the only types of jewellery. Amulets and Rings tend to drop less than other items, no matter how good they are.

To make things even harder, it's even less likely that you'll get a Legendary Amulet or Ring. Especially for new players who haven't finished the campaign or reached the level cap yet. The best way to get a Legendary early on is to move forward in the campaign. At the end of each Act, every player gets a Legendary. There is no way to know what Legendary it will be, so it will be hard to get an Amulet or Ring that can be used to make an Abstruse Sigil.

❖ *How to Use Abstruse Sigil*

Abstruse Sigil is used to make things, just like everything else. Herbs and ore are used to make potions and improve weapons and armour. Abstruse Sigil is used for something different. A Jeweller can use an Abstruse Sigil to improve the power of Legendary Amulets and Rings. The Jeweller is unlocked at Level 20 through a simple quest, so players won't have to wait long to use the Jeweler's services, which include the ability to take out gems that are already in sockets.

Even if you are below the level cap, you can use Abstruse Sigils to improve Legendary Amulets and Rings. But since Abstruse Sigils are hard to get at first, it's best for players to just hold on to them until the campaign is over. Even though upgrading equipment can be helpful, it is better to save rare materials like the Abstruse Sigil for the endgame, which is the part of the game that comes after the campaign.

As players get better and unlock more World Tiers, they'll get more Legendaries and find it easier to get and use Abstruse Sigils to make their builds even stronger.

How to Get Coiling Wards

❖ *How to Get Coiling Wards*

To get Coiling Wards, players must take to a Blacksmith legendary armour pieces with 400 or more Item Power that they want to sell. To be clear, armour pieces include helms, chests, gloves, legs, and boots, and salvaging them all gives you Coiling Wards. Also, players should make sure that the legendary armour pieces they are salvaging have the right Item Power, since less powerful items will only give lower-tier crafting materials in Diablo 4.

Even though most people will already know how to get Legendary items back in Diablo 4, a few words on the subject might help some. If a player wants to break down an item, all they have to do is go to a Blacksmith, which can be found in most towns and is marked on the map by an anvil, and click on the Salvage tab. Here, fans will see "Directly in Inventory" near the top of the menu. To salvage a Legendary, they should click the icon below "Directly in Inventory," choose the Legendary they want to salvage, and confirm.

At 400 Item Power, fans will also need to use Coiling Wards to imprint Aspects in Diablo 4. In fact, you only need Veiled Crystals, which are much easier to get than Coiling Wards, to put Aspects on items with 399 Item Power or less. So, players are told to keep imprinted items with Item Powers

just below 400 until they have found a reliable source of 400+ Legendary armour that can be salvaged.

For some fans, this means that they will have to wait until World Tier 3 to reach 400 Item Power. For those who don't know, Diablo 4 players can access World Tier 3 after they finish the campaign and the Cathedral of Light Capstone Dungeon, which is in World Tier 2. Even so, there are ways to get Legendaries before that point, and one of the best is to use Murmuring Obols to gamble at the Purveyor of Curiosities.

Where to Get Crushed Beast Bones

❖ *Crushed Beast Bones Location*

Diablo 4 players looking for Crushed Beast Bones should go to the Flooded Mine, a cellar in the Western Tunnels east of Margrave. For clarity, the exact location of this cellar has been marked on the map below, and fans coming from Margrave can quickly get there by climbing the nearby ladder. Even though it has only been tested in the Flooded Mine, the following farming method might work in other cellars as well.

When a player goes into the Flooded Mine, they should kill all of the enemies inside to make a chest appear. When this chest is opened, it seems to always give some number of Diablo 4 materials, usually four or five Crushed Beast Bones. If a player doesn't get the materials they need the first time they open the Flooded Mine chest, they should just leave the cellar, wait about two minutes for the event to respawn, and then go back in to try again.

Note that Diablo 4 players may have to do this process more than once before they have enough Crushed Beast Bones to upgrade the Light Healing Potion. Still, this seems to be a more reliable way to get the material than killing the animals that are all over the map. Some players say they have levelled up a lot by killing beasts in different places but have never seen a Crushed Beast Bone.

Still, if a player is determined to get Crushed Beast Bones by killing creatures, Scosglen seems to be the best place to go. Scosglen is a place in Diablo 4 that can be reached by going northeast from Kyovashad. There are a lot of beasts to fight there. Even though players who go after these beasts might not get their Crushed Beast Bones as quickly as those who go after the Flooded Mine cellar, they will at least be able to explore at the same time.

How to Get Baleful Fragments

You can get Baleful Fragments by dismantling Legendary weapons, which can be done at Diablo 4 Blacksmiths in many of the game's towns. Fans won't get Baleful Fragments every time they salvage a Legendary weapon, though, because these materials only come from weapons with 400+ Item Power. This means that players may have to work on their characters for a while to find a reliable source of Baleful Fragments.

It's important to note that 400 Item Power is also a key threshold for imprinting Aspects. In fact, you need Baleful Fragments, Coiling Wards, and another Rare Crafting Material to imprint Aspects on items with 400 Item Power or more. However, you only need Veiled Crystals to imprint Aspects on items with 399 Item Power or less. So, players should be careful when they go over 400 Item Power, because it might be a while before they have the materials they need to make their new items.

Since Legendary weapons are so important to getting Baleful Fragments, it seems like it would be useful to know how to get them. As a general rule, there are a few ways for players to try to get a lot of Legendaries, and farming World Events is probably the best of them. In fact, Legendaries can drop from the Elites that show up in these events, and fans will also get Diablo 4's Murmuring Obols when the events are over. Then, you can go to the Purveyor of Curiosities and spend these Obols to get more chances to get Legendary weapons.

Players can also try to farm for Diablo 4's legendary items in dungeons, where there are a lot of Elites. Dead Man's Dredge, which is near Yelesna and southeast of Kyovashad, is a great place for fans to go early in the game because there are a lot of Elites there. If a player wants to farm these Elites, they should just kill them, leave the dungeon, wait about two minutes for it to reset, and then do it all over again.

HOW TO DEFEAT ENEMIES AND BOSSES

How To Beat Ashava, The Pestilent

❖ *Location of Ashava, the Pestilent World Boss*

In the eastern part of the Fractured Peaks, there is a place called "The Crucible" where the fight against Ashava, the Pestilent takes place. The Bear Tribe Camp is the closest point on the map.

When the event is about to begin, a map icon with a timer will show up. The times for this world boss fight are already set, but Blizzard made two last-minute changes during the Early Access Beta. Players should listen for messages from Blizzard in case they have to do it again.

❖ *Requirements for the Ashava, the Pestilent Fight*

Defeating Ashava, the Pestilent is something that, in theory, anyone can do. Players don't have to do anything before they can play. So, characters should be around level 25 or higher to take on the fight. If not, you won't have enough DPS to kill it.

❖ *How to Beat Ashava, the Pestilent*

Ashava, The Pestilent is the boss in the Diablo 4 beta that players should look for if they want to fight the biggest and baddest boss in the game. It's impossible for a normal group of four people to beat this boss. Instead, Ashava spawns in a place that makes shards, which are copies of the zone where up to twelve people can fight together. Players just need to show up at the place to take part. The game will automatically put them in a shard with other players.

Players have two easy ways to give themselves the best chance of beating Ashava, the Pestilent World Boss:

- Get there early. Players should get into The Crucible zone with at least 10 minutes left on the clock. So, they can look around and see the other players they were put with. If even a few of the other players are below level 20, that shard probably won't win the fight. Players can go to a different shard by running out of the zone, waiting a few seconds, and then running back in.

- Bring down the world level. There is a low chance of being put into a group of level 25 players with good gear who can kill Ashava at World Tier 2 with only one chance. World Tier 1 is for players who want a better chance of winning.

Aside from these two things, the best way to get ready to fight Ashava is to learn how it attacks. Ashava doesn't have many moves, but the ones it does have are deadly. Here are all of Ashava's attacks and what you can do to avoid them.

Frost Swipe

The Frost Swipe could be Ashava's most dangerous attack. It hits a large area and does a ridiculous amount of Frost damage. It also does a lot of damage over time, which will need more than one potion to fix. You can either stand at Ashava's feet or far away from the swipe. Remember that Ashava always uses this attack twice, but not always in the same way. Sometimes it goes in a different direction, and sometimes it keeps going the same way.

Frost Rake

There are two parts to this attack. First, Ashava smashes the area in front of it with its huge claws. Then it rakes backwards to destroy anything on either side. When this hits you, it does a lot of damage right away and over time. If you stay in the middle of Ashava's back feet, you can avoid it.

Plague Belch

When Ashava uses Plague Belch, it spews a cloud of disgusting plague juice in front of it. It does a lot of damage over time and leaves behind a big pool of plague juice. Try to avoid the puddle as much as possible, but if you don't want to go all the way around it, you can dodge through it.

○ *The Noob Squasher*

The Noob Squasher is the easiest move to see and gives you a lot of time to get away. Ashava raises its huge fist, waits for a second, and then slams it down in the yellow circle area. It's not Ashava's most powerful attack, but it can kill low-armor characters in one hit.

○ *Ashava Chomp*

It would be best for players not to stand around in front of Ashava. When it sees a player in front of it, it bites down on them. Ashava's Chomp does a lot of damage, but it doesn't always kill in one hit. So they don't get hit by this attack, players should stay near Ashava's feet or sides.

Ashava can't move around very well. It can't just run all over the field. But Ashava can sometimes jump across the pitch. Ashava is a slow-moving target, except when it jumps. To win, you have to avoid attacks and keep your DPS high for a long time. If players can do that, Ashava, the Pestilent will die and they'll get their rewards.

How to Beat Astaroth

❖ *In Diablo 4, who is Astaroth?*

In Act 2 of Diablo 4, Astaroth will be a part of what happens. Lilith brings it back to life, and then they make a deal: Lilith gets to go back to Hell, and the demon can burn down anyone who tries to stop a demon lord from coming back.

Astaroth is especially close to Donan, one of the player's most important allies, because he was one of the few people who managed to seal the demon away in the first place. Since the demon's return meant that Doran's son had to die, players will have the chance to get even with him in this final battle.

Astaroth doesn't want to fight the player one-on-one as a boss. Instead, the demon rides a companion demon into battle, which is dangerous on many fronts. Because this enemy is so big, there isn't usually much room to work with. Players will have to be smart about where they stand and how they use their skills to avoid getting hurt and keep the pressure on.

This is important if you want to deal with Astaroth's attacks, which include:

- If a player gets too close, they should move to the side or back away to stay safe.

- Blowing on the three heads of the demon dog will make fire streams come out. Move to the side to avoid getting hurt and attack Astaroth freely.

- AoE damage from projectiles. Danger spots are marked, so stay away from them and keep your attention on Astaroth.

- As Astaroth's health goes down, meteors fall from the sky and start a new attack. In the same way, stay out of their impact zone.

- In the last part of the level, the boss will get more aggressive and use all of these attacks in quick succession. It's important to keep doing damage and even take some yourself if that means killing the boss early.

With enough patience, better gear, and a lot of healing potions, the player will eventually kill Astaroth. Then, they can go after Lilith and stop her evil plans.

How to Beat Genbar & Mahmon

❖ *Who are Genbar and Mahmon?*

Genbar and Mahmon are not names that come to mind when you think of the series, like many of the other characters you will meet in the game. That's because they're brand new to the series, but they're still problems that need to be solved. Players should be around level 43 to 47 at this point.

During Acts 2 and 3, players will try to find Genbar, a well-known woodcarver, to find out where Elias and Lilith are. When you go to his workshop, though, you'll see that he's been influenced by Lilith and is now willing to kill for the Mother. In the end, Mahmon shows up as a surprise guest.

❖ *Diablo 4: How to Beat Genbar and Mahmon*

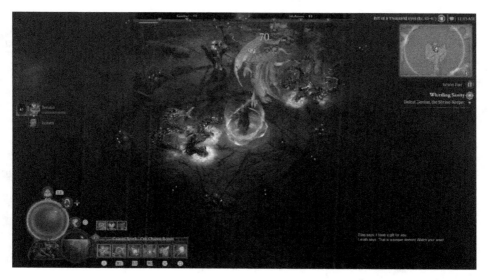

Even if a Diablo 4 player is playing alone, they won't be alone during this boss fight because Lorath will be going with them to find Genbar. Genbar will be the only opponent when things start, and he will be the only one who can fight close up. However, he is more dangerous at a distance with his demonic spells.

Kite the boss as he throws things at you and take care of the smaller demons he can call up. Getting him close to half health shouldn't be too hard, and then things will start to get interesting. Elias will use his magic to give Mahmon to Genbar as a gift. Mahmon is a demon that was called to even things out.

Think of Mahmon as a more powerful Pit Lord. Its huge body and swinging weapon can do a lot of damage. Things are going to get busier, but the key is to focus on one boss at a time and take them out first. Genbar is the main target, so keep attacking the woodcarver and use spells, traps, and skills to stun either one or both bosses at the same time to keep your health up.

This will keep more enemies from joining the fight, and once Genbar is dead the fight with Mahmon will be a war of attrition. Again, skills and spells that weaken the demon work very well against it. If Lorath draws its attention, you can attack from a distance to avoid any danger.

If you know how to use your numbers and the battlefield well, it won't take long to beat the two of them. The road to Lilith is still long and dangerous, so grab all the loot and look for upgrades if you need to.

How to Beat Andariel, Maiden of Anguish

❖ *In Diablo 4, who is Andariel?*

The Maiden of Anguish is a familiar face for long-time fans of the series. She first showed up in Diablo 2 as a Lesser Evil. Her brother, Duriel, is also a dangerous Lesser Evil. She would be mentioned in later adventures, but it wouldn't be until Diablo 4 that she would come back in a big way.

After the events of Acts 3 and 4, Elias is able to call her, and it's now up to the player to kill her and stop a new Reign of Anguish.

❖ *Diablo 4: How to Beat Andariel*

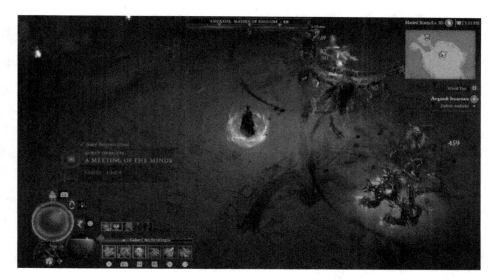

Before the fight even starts, it's a good idea to know what the players can and can't do. In Diablo 4, the fight against Andariel doesn't take place in the open overworld or even in a dungeon. Instead, it takes place in a small arena where sandstorms are raging. If you touch the sand, it will hurt you for a long time, so stay away from the edges.

❖ *Andariel Boss Fight Stage 1*

At the start of the fight, Andariel shows up as a chained-up opponent, which gives her a few ways to hurt her opponent. Among these are:

- Using Rune Chains, which can bind and slow down players in an area, to cast them. To be free, you have to break the Rune Chains.

- AoE attacks that look like red lines will quickly kill the player, so stay away from them at all costs. Watch out for branching lines, too, because they can catch you off guard if you're not paying attention.

- Andariel will also move around the arena by teleporting, leaving projectiles behind her. Look at the minimap to find out where she is.

Whenever she attacks, use whatever chance you have to deal damage to her and avoid taking damage yourself. When she uses AoE attacks, she also leaves herself open to long-term damage. Upgrade your gear and skills to keep up the pressure, and she will soon move on to the next phase.

❖ Andariel Boss Fight Stage 2

Andariel will break free of her chains once the first part of her health is gone She will then grow those familiar appendages and use new attacks in addition to the ones she already knows. Among them are:

- If she gets close and swipes you with her pincers, either dash behind her or stay far away to avoid damage.

- She can also attack from both sides with an extended chain, so watch for the sign and move out of the way.

The boss will get more aggressive, so use healing potions sparingly and use all of your skills to get rid of as much of her health as quickly as possible.

How to Beat Mohlon, Snake Queen

❖ Getting to Mohlon

Once a player has the goal of getting to Yngovani, which is in Hawezar, they need to find two eyes for the Serpent Wall. One is at a Destroyed Serpent Shrine on the eastern side of the swamp, while the other is in the hands of a dying bandit in the far north.

Go back to the Serpent Wall with both eyes and put them in. This will open the way to the Serpent's Lair. Make sure to upgrade the right gear and make some anti-poison potions before the fight.

❖ How to Beat Mohlon

Mohlon, the Snake Queen, will come out to play once the Incense Box in the lair is turned on. As a snake, she will use a lot of poisonous attacks that can easily kill anyone who isn't ready. Make sure you have the right equipment and gear, like an Elixir of Poison Resistance, for defence and offence.

Some of her attacks to avoid are:

- It makes a wide attack with its tail, so move to the back to avoid getting hurt badly.

- An attack that uses poisonous spit as a projectile. This can be fixed by moving the spit to the left or right.

As Mohlon's health goes down, her attacks tend to get stronger, and she will also call on other enemies to help her as the fight goes on. If you can, get rid of all the eggs around the small arena, and watch out for more snakes that might join the party. In the later stages, AoE damage will be useful, so use skills that can do that a lot.

After defeating the Snake Queen, open the chest to get the Mystic Incense, which you can bring to Taissa to continue the main storyline of Diablo 4.

How to Beat Valtha, Witch of the Wastes

❖ *Diablo 4: How to Find Valtha*

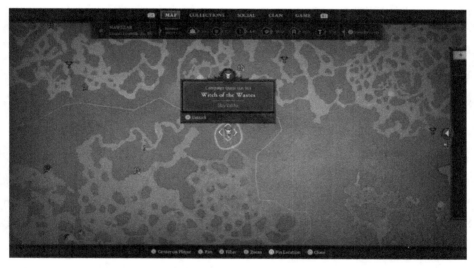

As was said, the goal of location Valtha will be given to players in Act 5. From the Ruined Tower in Wejinhani, which is in the Hawezar region, head northeast towards the Cinder Wastes. At some point, you will be able to see Valtha's Hovel. Check out the Manifesto and Valtha's Spellbook for hints about where Purified Quicksilver might be.

When you do these things, the witch will show up at her house. After some harsh threats, the boss fight will start.

❖ *Diablo 4: How to Beat Valtha*

Since Valtha is a witch, players can expect to get hit with a lot of magical attacks while fighting her. This makes her move slowly, and her conjuration takes a while to work. This makes it easier for players to hit her while she is trying to dodge.

Her biggest attack is the meteors she can call down, so move out of the circles on the ground to avoid damage and keep focusing on Valtha with powerful skills that become available as you level up. She can also throw fireballs that head straight for you, so move away to throw them off the trail. Get out of the way when you see a thick line on the ground to avoid the firewall.

At some point, the witch will start calling in mobs to help her. Focus on these outsiders and get rid of them before going back to attack Valtha. At the end of the fight, it makes more sense to focus on Valtha to end it as quickly as possible. This is so that we don't get too busy with the growing number of mobs that are being called.

When you beat the boss, she will drop the Vial of Purified Quicksilver, which you can take back to the Ruined Tower to continue the story.

How to Beat Elias, Fallen Horadrim

❖ In Diablo 4, who is Elias?

During the whole game, players will start to find out more about Elias. Lorath will say that he used to be a disciple who was obsessed with getting more knowledge and power and wasn't always happy with how the Horadrim were doing things.

Elias's actions in Diablo 4 set things in motion. He had dreams of a better future with Lilith in charge. That puts the players on a path to run into this skilled enemy.

❖ Diablo 4: How to Beat Elias

To defeat this enemy, you need to know how hard it is to do what you need to do. Players will fight Elias more than once, but since he is immortal, it is impossible to beat him—at least, until the secret to his immortality is found.

❖ Fighting Elias in Act 3

During the Piercing the Veil objective, players will go to the temple of Lilith and finally meet the mysterious Pale Man, who dies way too easily. As expected, this isn't the last time you'll see him. In fact, there are two more times you'll meet him in the temple.

Instead of being the biggest threat, the mobs that help Elias are, especially for solo players, the biggest danger in this Act. He will get away in the end and live to see another day.

❖ Fighting Elias in Act 5

After Elias's finger is burned, he is no longer immortal, and Act 5: On the Precipice is where the real battle starts. Elias is a dangerous enemy because he has powerful magical attacks and can call on strong mobs to do his bidding. Players will always have to be aware of where they are on the battlefield and divide their attention to even the odds as much as possible.

His usual ranged attacks can be avoided, but that's not the biggest problem. There are two important AoE attacks. The first is a wide cone of blood that hits hard in front of Elias. If you can, move to the side. Next, blood vapours are used to cover a large area of the ground, which makes it easier to hit multiple times. This attack will always hit, so use healing potions to make sure your health is at its best before going on the attack.

Mobs that are summoned are also dangerous, and Pit Lords and Oppressors are part of the fun. Use strong skills to take them out quickly and turn everyone's attention back to Elias. With any luck, the lost Horadrim will be killed, and Diablo 4's endgame will be here soon.

How to Beat Duriel, Lord of Pain

❖ Who is Duriel in Diablo 4?

Duriel is a Lesser Evil, much like his sister Andariel. As the Lord of Pain, it's clear that this demon is happy to bring about the end of humanity and kill anyone who gets in its way. Duriel used to be a loyal servant of Diablo, but in Diablo 4, he shows up as one of Lilith's main generals and must be killed for the story to move forward.

❖ Diablo 4: How to Beat Duriel

In the last part of Diablo 4, Duriel will get in the way of finding a way into Hell, where Lilith is working on the next step of her plans. Duriel is a sight to see, what with its huge size and scary blades for arms.

Attacks that stand out are:

- When it burrows into the ground, it can't be hurt, and when it comes back up, it's in a better position. Use the time to get better and heal up before the battle starts up again.

- Duriel's poisonous puke can cause a lot of trouble in the arena, so try to stay away from the pools and move around the demon to spread out its attacks as much as possible.

- Duriel can also eat the player, which does a lot of damage. He shows that he's about to do this by stomping, so move away from him and get ready to dodge left or right.

Aside from these attacks, Duriel is a tough opponent, which makes the battle even harder. For melee characters like Druids and Barbarians, make sure to stay on the move to avoid their normal attacks. Keep your Rogue or Sorcerer healthy if you want them to stay in the fight. Bring down the Lesser Evil, and it will be much easier to get to Lilith.

Basic How To's and Questions Answered

How To Change Controls & Bind Custom Keys

Diablo 4 is very well made for console play, and many players, even PC players, now prefer to play Sanctuary with a gamepad instead of a mouse and keyboard. It's easier to move around the world, and it's easier on the hands. Long-range attacks are less precise, but close-range combat is more fun. The UI is not easier to use with a controller.

Console players can't just click on each menu tab in order to get to the keybindings page quickly when they want to change how the controls work in Diablo 4. First, use the Select button on Xbox or the Share button on PlayStation to open the Map. Then, use the shoulder buttons on either type of controller to get to the Game Menu.

Then, scroll down and open the Options menu. Use the shoulders again to get to the Controls tab on the top bar. To change how actions in Diablo 4 are mapped to a controller, players must find each action they want to change, scroll to the right of it, and click the box that shows the action's current button. The box will be highlighted, and the next controller input will be used for that action instead.

Even though Xbox and PlayStation players have to rebind their controls one at a time with their controller, PC players who use a controller can still use the keyboard and mouse interface to make the process a bit easier. The game automatically switches between the controller and the keyboard and mouse when either is used.

How to Play With Friends

❖ *How Multiplayer Works*

The always-online multiplayer system in Diablo 4 is interesting, but it means that even people who want to play single-player may have to wait a long time. Even outside of towns, there are a lot of other players in the world. People are running around killing and opening the same enemies and chests. But it's good that loot drops differently for each person.

In Diablo 4, people who play together get a bonus. Just being close to another player gives you a buff that gives you an extra 5% XP. This makes it worth your time to help people. If players are in a party, they get a 10% XP bonus instead, which makes it a good idea to work together.

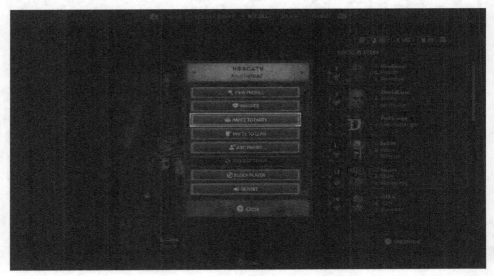

Cross-play is an option for players who want to play with people from other platforms. Under "Social" in the Options Menu, players can choose to turn off cross-play if they want to. At the end of the list, there is a setting called "Quick Join" that lets friends join the party without being invited.

Here's how to get a group of people together online to play Diablo 4:

1. Click on the "Social" tab in the Game Menu.

2. If they aren't already on the Friends List, choose "Add a Friend" to add a friend's BattleTag.

3. Choose the friend you want to invite, and then click Invite to Party.

Here's how to play Diablo 4 with a friend at the same console:

1. Make two characters for Diablo 4, one for each player.

2. Hook up a second controller to the console and press the Start button on that controller.

3. Let each player choose a character.

4. Choose to play.

❖ *Troubleshooting*

There are a few possible reasons why Diablo 4 players might not be able to connect with other people. Here are a few things that could be done:

1. If players can't see someone on their local network, they should go to the Options menu and scroll to the bottom of the "Social" tab. Turn on the setting called "Enable Display of Local Network Players."

2. If friends aren't showing up as online in the Friends List, make sure they aren't set to "Appear Offline." If they are, you won't be able to invite them to the party.

3. If couch co-op isn't working, you should finish the Prologue and try again. Blizzard has confirmed that there are problems with couch co-op in the Prologue.

How To Pet The Dog

In Diablo 4, the first step to petting a dog is to find one. Nearly every settlement that turns off combat skills has at least one dog lurking around, usually near NPCs. But when a player walks up to one, it doesn't do anything, and there's no prompt to pet it like there is in other games.

Wait until the dog stops moving. It will stand still for a few seconds before going somewhere else. Make sure your character is basically touching the dog and facing it. It doesn't matter which way the dog is facing, though.

Lastly, bring up the emote wheel by pressing E on the mouse or keyboard or up on the D-Pad on a controller and choose the "Hello" emote. Verify the emote, and then leave the wheel. If the player's character is facing the dog, they will say hello to it while bending down to scratch it.

This doesn't give the player any bonuses or anything, but it's always nice to play with man's best friend, especially in a game as dark as Diablo 4. It's worth checking out during the last few days of beta testing or when the full game comes out on June 6, 2023 (or a few days earlier for those who preordered).

How to Level Up Fast

To level up quickly in Sanctuary, players will need to do a lot of different things. Dungeons, Renown Rewards, and Side Quests are some of the best ways. Diablo 4 gives out a lot of XP, so it doesn't take much to do optimisation right. So, the tips below will help players get the most out of their games.

❖ *Play at a Higher World Tier*

The player's choice of World Tier affects a lot of things, like how many enemies appear, how strong they are, how hard they hit, and more. But for every buff the enemies get, the player gets a huge boost in XP and the quality of their loot. The bigger the reward, the more difficult the task.

❖ Use Potions

There are a lot of elixirs that give extra Experience. Alchemists can make these elixirs, which need certain ingredients that can be found all over Sanctuary. Pick the best elixirs for your Diablo 4 build and buy a lot of them. Then, when you go into a dungeon or take part in a world event, drink a potion to get more experience from it.

❖ Play with Friends

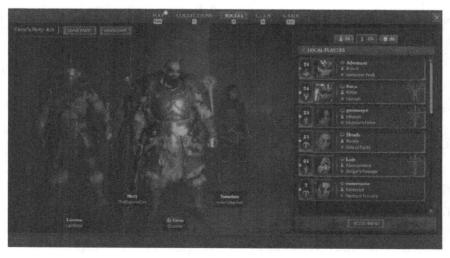

Blizzard decided to give players more XP if they play Diablo 4 with a group. This was done to get more people to play together. Everything gives players in a party 10% more XP. You also get an extra 5% XP if you're near another player, even if they're not in your party.

❖ Complete Side Missions

People live in every outpost on the map because they need something. Some ask the wanderer to help them find food in the woods, while others want the wanderer to take the head off of a hideous monster. Some mission givers, like Sister Octavia, offer more than one mission. She can be found on the east side of Kyovashad. If you finish these missions, you'll get a lot of extra XP.

❖ Clear Side Dungeons

In Diablo 4, the Side Dungeons give cool rewards called Aspects. Aspects are enchantments that players can unlock and use with any character on their account. They're hard, full of creatures, and always end with an epic boss battle. If players go from one dungeon to the next with their friends, they can gain levels quickly.

❖ Earn Renown Rewards

Diablo 4 keeps track of how far along players are in each area of the map. As the player does side quests, dungeons, and other things, they will earn Renown for that region. Players can get rewards when they reach certain levels of Renown. These give a lot of Bonus XP, but remember that to get to the higher tiers, you have to play at a higher World Tier.

How to Cheer

❖ How to Use the Emote Wheel

Diablo 4 has a built-in emote wheel that helps players talk to each other. This is similar to what many online games like Overwatch 2, Destiny 2, and a lot of others have. Players with a PC can get to it by pressing the "E" key on their keyboard, while those with a console or controller can choose "Up" on the D-Pad. By default, the emote wheel can hold up to eight options at once. These include actions like waving, following, and saying "thanks," as well as more emotional options like saying "sorry" or "teasing." Choose the option from the wheel to have the player character do the emote and say the voice line that goes with it.

❖ How to Complete the Raising Spirits Quest with Cheer

Now that players know how to use the emote wheel in Diablo 4, it's time to put that knowledge to good use because it will be needed in a couple of missions. The first is the Secret of the Springs quest, which is a traditional "go here and kill" quest with some puzzles and emotes added. But that one is pretty easy, since you just need to use the "Wait" emote, which is easy to find on the Emote Wheel.

Once players get to the town of Kyovashad, though, they will eventually start the Raising Spirits quest. After talking to an NPC guard named Boza, the player will need to go to the training barracks in town to cheer up the soldiers who are stationed there. To do that, players will need to use the Cheer emote, which isn't normally on the wheel.

At this point, players will have to open their Emote Wheel, customise it, find the "Cheer" emote, and add it to the wheel. There are a lot of emote options in Diablo 4, but the wheel can only hold a certain number of them. This means that players can pick and add the ones they want. Once "Cheer" has been assigned and saved, use it on the group of soldiers standing at the blue icon on the minimap to finish that part of the quest. Go back to Boza to get your XP and money for doing a good job.

How to Start a Clan

❖ How to Start a Clan

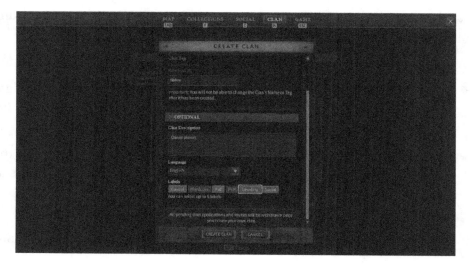

In Diablo 4, a clan is a way for players who like the same things and play the same way to get together. It can be open to the public to get certain players to join, or it can be closed to people who already know who they want to play with.

To start a clan in Diablo 4, players don't have to finish any story parts or talk to any NPCs. It can be done whenever and wherever. Here's what to do first:

1. Open the Game Menu and go to the "Clan" tab.

2. Choose to make a clan.

3. In the Clan Name field, type a name for the clan.

4. In the Clan Tag field, type a tag for the clan. It can be as long as six characters.

5. Clan Description, Language, and Label are all optional, but players should fill these out if this will be a public clan. It's a good place to talk about things like whether people in this clan will skip the story or what difficulty they like to play on.

6. Once everything is set up right, click Create Clan.

❖ *How to Customize a Clan*

When the clan is set up right, players will be able to find it and find it useful when they do. There are ranks that can be given to players, messages that can be shown, a banner that can be changed, and more. It's pretty strong but also easy to use.

When you choose Manage Clan from the Clan Menu, another menu pops up:

- The "Summary" tab opens first. Here, players can change the Visibility, Message of the Day, Labels, and more. This tab also has buttons for players to use if they want to leave their clan or break up their clan.

- Players can change what each rank in the clan is allowed to do on the "Permissions" tab. This includes things like who can talk in voice chat and who can move members up or down the ranks.

- On the "Heraldry" tab, the leader of the clan can change how a banner looks. From the menu, you can change the background, the symbols, and the colours. If a player is having trouble coming up with ideas, they can use the button "Randomise All" to get some inspiration.

- The final tab is called "Bans." We hope these won't be needed, but if a player gets kicked out, their name will be there. Players with the right rank can change bans whenever they need to.

What is Hardcore Mode?

Since Diablo 2, players have been able to play a version of the game called Hardcore Mode that is very hard and dangerous. In Hardcore Mode, if a player dies, his or her character is gone for good. There is no way to come back from death, and there are no second chances like there are in the regular game. This mode was popular enough that it was added to Diablo 3 when it came out, and there was even a trophy/achievement for killing certain bosses while playing on Hardcore Mode. Hardcore Mode will, of course, come back for Diablo 4.

Players only have one life, so they have to be very careful when they are exploring Sanctuary and trying to figure out what Lilith is up to. If Diablo 4 players aren't careful, all it takes is one bad encounter with the Butcher or going into an unprepared dungeon for them to lose their character and have to start over from the beginning.

Hardcore Mode is dangerous, but players don't have to face them alone. Players don't have to go through this mode by themselves; they can bring their friends along to make it easier to handle. One important thing to know about Diablo 4 is that death is still permanent in Hardcore Mode, even when playing PvP. So, if players want to do PvP in Hardcore Mode, they should come with a group and be ready for the worst.

❖ Are There Any Rewards for Playing Hardcore Mode?

Even though the main reward for beating Hardcore Mode is being able to brag about it, players who are brave enough to face its dangers can also get some more tangible rewards. Players will get unique titles that they can't get any other way if they reach certain levels and kill story-related bosses. Even killing players in PvP while playing in Hardcore Mode can earn you a title.

Players can also get a special reward that is only available for a certain amount of time. The names of the first 1,000 people to reach Level 100 in

Hardcore Mode will be carved into a statue of Lilith.

How to Switch Weapons

All of the classes in the game, except for the Barbarian, can switch weapons without having to do anything. A Rogue, for example, can use daggers to attack up close, but will switch to a bow when the skill needs a ranged component. As for the Barbarian, the unique way the class fights will be more useful in Diablo 4 when it comes to switching weapons.

This is because Barbarians can use up to four weapons, including two sets of two-handed weapons and two one-handed weapons. These weapons can either belong to the slashing or bludgeoning school of skills. Even though some skills will automatically switch between all of the weapons in the Barbarian's arsenal, some skills can be set to use a specific weapon to do the dirty job.

Open the Skills Menu to make sure that the chosen weapon is linked to a certain skill. To change a skill, move the cursor to the skill that needs to be changed and press the middle mouse button on a PC to see all the weapons that can be used for that skill. For console players, you have to assign the skill to the quickbar, and there will be a key to press to switch between weapons.

When the Barbarian fights against the forces of evil in Diablo 4, choosing the right weapons to go with the right skills is more than just a matter of style. One of the many improvements made to the game is that it now has more strategic depth and more tactical flexibility. This will likely allow players to customise their builds even more when the game goes live in just a few months.

How To Dodge

❖ *Evade Is New – And Important – in Diablo 4*

The Evade mechanic is new to Diablo 4, but avoiding enemies and dodging attacks has always been a part of how the games are played. For example, the Sorceress's Teleport skill is one of many that is often used to avoid attacks in the other games. But in Diablo 4, all classes have a button that lets them dodge. This is very helpful when fighting bosses and getting out of tight spots.

Players who are used to I-frames from the Souls series might be disappointed to find out that the Evade feature in Diablo 4 is different. When a player uses Evade, they can still be hit by attacks they collide with, but enemies won't be able to hit them because Evade makes them pass through them. To make the most of this ability, you should time your Evades to get out of the way of attacks, not to dodge through them.

❖ *How To Dodge*

By default, players must press the Space button on PC, the B button on Xbox, or the Circle button on PlayStation to Evade. The player's character will move quickly in the direction they are facing, and the player's Evade ability will stop working. When players Evade, they don't run into enemies, so it's a good way to get out of a tight spot.

If a player doesn't have any gear that changes the ability, Evade will become usable again after five seconds. Different Boots will give Evade different buffs, such as more charges, a speed boost when it's used, and a shorter cooldown depending on the attack.

As evading is one of the most important parts of Diablo 4, players should get to know it well. At higher World Tiers, it's important to know how to use the Evade ability so that the player doesn't get hit by everything that comes their way.

How To Increase Stash

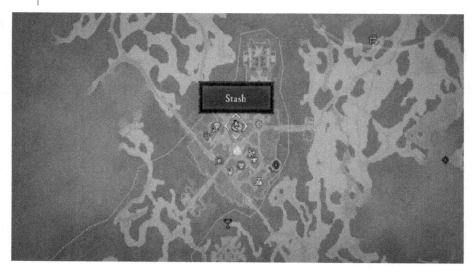

In Diablo 4, the Stash is a shared inventory space with 50 slots that can be used by more than one character. To make it bigger, players have to go to the Stash and follow the on-screen instructions to trade their gold for more tabs.

This feature can be used for the first time as soon as a player gets to Kyovashad, the game's first major hub city. Within that city, players only need to mark the chest-shaped icon on their Diablo 4 map and follow the path to it. In Kyovashad in particular, the chest is right next to a wardrobe where players can change how they look.

The first increase to the Stash in Diablo 4 costs 100,000 gold. This is a lot of money for new players, which suggests that it might not be important to increase the Stash capacity until after the First Act is over. But Blizzard is known for overpricing rewards in games like Diablo 4, so it's possible that this high initial cost is meant to keep players grinding for longer than they need to in the beginning areas.

As the Early Access phase of Diablo 4 comes to an end, features like the in-game Stash have been well received. No matter how much it cost, making the Stash hold more items has helped the game get a lot of positive feedback just like many other "quality of life" changes.

When everyone can play Diablo 4, time will tell if this good buzz will be ruined by the increased stress on the Diablo 4 servers or by the release of Sanctuary's first Battle Pass.

How To Respec

❖ How To Respec Skill Points

In Diablo 4, players can change their class right from the skill menu. They don't have to talk to an old woman at the Encampment or be in a town centre or other safe place. Open your inventory anywhere in the world and click on the "ABILITIES" tab to see the skills and abilities menu. Here, players can see what skills and passives they have chosen.

In Diablo 4, players can change where their skill points go by either taking them all back at once or one at a time. By returning all of their points at once, players can start over and redistribute their points starting from the top Basic Skills category. However, a clean slate isn't always what's needed to make a build better.

To make changes to a build instead of resetting it, scroll over an ability that no longer fits and right-click on PC or hold down the refund button prompt on console. This takes away one skill point from the chosen ability. If the skill point is needed for other abilities, it won't be taken away.

When respeccing one skill point at a time in Diablo 4, start at the bottom and work your way up. Also, don't forget to remove skill points from secondary modifiers for abilities.

❖ *Respeccing Costs Gold*

It's easy to change your specialisation in Diablo 4, but that ease comes at a price – literally. In Diablo 4, players can return and redistribute skill points as much as they want for the first ten levels, though they don't have a lot of options. This lets players get a feel for what their class is like, but after they reach level 10, they have to pay gold to change their class.

The price is not crazy high, at least not at first. From level 10 to level 20, players won't notice much of an effect on their bank accounts. The character in the picture above is level 23, when it costs about 78 Gold to refund each point.

But the cost of getting back skill points goes up as a player spends more time in their class tree. By max level, players can expect to pay thousands of gold to refund just one point and hundreds of thousands to completely respec into the best builds in Diablo 4.

This is not just about the skill points you get when you level up. When players spend skill points they've earned from quests, acts, and the paragon points system, prices will go up. Players have a lot of time to learn about their class and try out different options, but as they get closer to max level, it's best to choose a build to avoid these endgame costs.

WEAPONS, ARMOR, AND MORE

HOW TO TRANSMOG & CHANGE CHARACTER APPEARANCE

How To Transmog

- Talk to the Wardrobe. An icon will show up on the map.

- Choose the 'Wardrobe' option.

Players will need to be in a major city or outpost to find a wardrobe. If a player wants to start this process early, they will have to do the first few quests in the journal. Luckily, they should be able to do this within an hour. You don't have to reach the highest level before you start this process.

When you choose an item from the wardrobe, a list of transmogrification options will appear. On this same screen, players can also match their outfits to a single colour scheme if they want to look like they go together. Keep in mind that players can only change their gear into styles they've already unlocked, and not all pieces of gear can be changed to a different colour.

How To Change Appearance

- Talk to the Wardrobe.

- Choose the 'Appearance' option.

Changing your appearance is even easier and can be done in the same place as transmogrification. Choose "Appearance" from the second tab in the wardrobe. This will give players a setup that is similar to what was used when the character was made.

As players move through the World Tiers, they may find that a different look goes better with a certain type of gear. Some hairstyles look silly when worn with a certain helm. If this happens, it's up to you to make the necessary changes.

How To Unlock More Transmog Options

- Find a piece of gear that says "Unlocks new look on salvage" on it.

- Get a blacksmith to try to fix the piece.

At first, players can only change what they are wearing by putting on rags. Some players might think about switching classes so they don't look so bad, but it takes all of them a while to look good enough to go out in public.

Go to a blacksmith and look for an icon that says the item will give you a new way to change your look. Have them find a way to use the old piece in the new design and collect some crafting materials.

HOW TO IMPROVE GEAR

In Diablo 4, players have a lot more ways to improve their gear than they did in previous games. The following shops can help players improve their gear:

- Arms and weapons can be fixed and improved by a blacksmith.

- Occultists can do Enchantments and pull out and imprint Aspects.

- Jeweller: Can change the level of jewellery, add sockets to gear, make Gems, and take them out of sockets.

Upgrades

The easiest way to improve gear is to do a "Upgrade" on it, which just means using parts and gold to improve its stats. Based on how rare it is, each item can only be upgraded a certain number of times. The upgrades also cost more gold and parts as they go on.

Upgrading is a great way for players to improve gear that they plan to keep for a long time. But since resources and gold are expensive, it would be a waste to use them on a piece that might be replaced soon.

Enchantments

In Diablo 4, affixes are what give gear its different stat bonuses. If a player doesn't like an affix on a piece of gear, they can Enchant it by going to the Occultist. They will get to choose one of three random affixes to put in its place. The third choice is sometimes to keep the original affix. Once an affix on a piece of equipment has been enchanted, it can no longer be changed.

The price to enchant an item goes up the more rare it is. If a player wants to make an item legendary by adding an Aspect to it, they should first finish any enchantments that item needs. This will keep them from having to waste more valuable materials.

Aspects

The extraction and imprinting of Aspects is another service that the Occultist offers. These are great spells that can be used in a lot of different ways. You can get them from legendary gear or open the Codex of Power to find out how to get them. The ones from gear can only be used once, but the ones from the Codex of Power can be used over and over again by any character.

Each Aspect can only be used with certain kinds of gear. Many of them can be put on different kinds of gear, but some can only be put on certain things, like weapons or jewellery. The amount of power they have varies a lot, so two versions of the same Aspect can have very different values.

When a player takes an Aspect out of an item, the item it came from is destroyed. When you imprint an Aspect on an item, it not only makes it legendary but also changes its look a lot to match its new level of awesomeness. There is a fee for these services, but it doesn't cost much in terms of resources and gold.

Gems

The Gem system in Diablo 4 is a lot like the Gem systems in the previous games. The Jeweller can put together gems that aren't as strong to make ones that are. They can also add and remove gem sockets from gear as needed. In neither case does the gear change. It takes a little bit of resources but nothing is lost.

You can only add one socket to a piece of gear, even if it already has one. But even one gem can make a big difference. The Chipped Skull, for example, gives +13 Life on Kill, +5% Healing Received, or +170 Armour when it's slotted into weapons, armour, or jewellery, respectively.

HOW TO SWAP WEAPONS

All of the classes in the game, except for the Barbarian, can switch weapons without having to do anything. A Rogue, for example, can use daggers to attack up close, but will switch to a bow when the skill needs a ranged component. As for the Barbarian, the unique way the class fights will be more useful in Diablo 4 when it comes to switching weapons.

This is because Barbarians can use up to four weapons, including two sets of two-handed weapons and two one-handed weapons. These weapons can either belong to the slashing or bludgeoning school of skills. Even though some skills will automatically switch between all of the weapons in the Barbarian's arsenal, some skills can be set to use a specific weapon to do the dirty job.

Open the Skills Menu to make sure that the chosen weapon is linked to a certain skill. To change a skill, move the cursor to the skill that needs to be changed and press the middle mouse button on a PC to see all the weapons that can be used for that skill. For console players, you have to assign the skill to the quickbar, and there will be a key to press to switch between weapons.

When the Barbarian fights against the forces of evil in Diablo 4, choosing the right weapons to go with the right skills is more than just a matter of style. One of the many improvements made to the game is that it now has more strategic depth and more tactical flexibility. This will likely allow players to customise their builds even more when the game goes live in just a few months.

HOW TO SALVAGE GEAR

What is Gear Salvaging?

Like in loot-based games like Destiny 2 or Borderlands 3, players will find a lot of gear and weapons that they can only store in a backpack or some other small container. When exploring or doing quests in Diablo 4, you can quickly run out of space in your inventory. Knowing how to Salvage gear can be a lifesaver for freeing up space and getting important crafting materials.

Reusing gear is also an important part of Diablo 4's transmog, which lets you change the way your gear looks. Salvaged gear gives weapons and armour new looks. This gives players more ways to change how they look, especially if a good weapon or piece of armour doesn't have the look they want. Players should also pay attention to the item descriptions, which say if the look can be unlocked by salvaging or not.

How to Salvage Gear and Items

Even though gear salvaging is talked about a lot in Diablo 4, players won't be able to do it until they get to the city of Kyovashad and find the Blacksmith. The Blacksmith is marked on the map by an anvil, and players can either sell their gear to them for gold or salvage it to get materials and a new look.

The first tab in the Blacksmith is the Salvage screen, which gives players these choices:

- Salvage all junk: Players can mark gear in their inventory as junk, so choosing this option will automatically salvage all of them.

- Common: Bring back all items of common (white) quality.

- Magic - Salvage all magic (blue) quality items.

- Rare: Sell all items of rare (yellow) quality.

- All Items: This option salvages everything in the player's backpack except for legendary-tier items.

The top also has a pickaxe icon that lets players salvage items from their inventory one at a time instead of all at once like the other options.

HOW TO GET BLADEDANCER'S ASPECT

Stemming the Flow, a main story quest that shows up in Act 2, must be done before Bladedancer's Aspect can be unlocked. More specifically, the quest becomes available around the middle of the act. Players can easily meet this requirement by following the waypoints in the Campaign section of their Journals.

Once Stemming the Flow is over, players should go to Jalal's Vigil, a dungeon in the northeast corner of Scosglen. The exact location of this dungeon is shown on the map below, and fans will be able to get Bladedancer's Aspect when they beat the boss at the end of the dungeon.

In terms of what Bladedancer's Aspect does, it makes the Rogue's Twisting Blades Core Skill even stronger. More specifically, it makes the blades orbit the Diablo 4 Rogue for a short time after they come back to them. This hurts enemies nearby. This damage is based on the return damage and range of Twisting Blades, and the Aspect is a key part of builds that use that skill a lot

Twisting Blades Rogue is thought to be one of the best builds in Diablo 4 at the moment, both for levelling up and for the end game. This is why Bladedancer's Aspect is so popular, and Rogue players should definitely think about trying it out. This isn't the only strong Rogue build in the game, though. Fans can also build around skills like Flurry, Penetrating Shot, and Barrage to get good results.

Last but not least, Bladedancer's Aspect is an Offensive Aspect, which means it can only be imprinted on weapons, amulets, rings, and gloves. If the player plans to use this Diablo 4 Aspect while levelling up, it's best that they don't imprint it on their weapons, since they're likely to get new ones often as they go through the campaign. Fans are instead told to put Bladedancer's Aspect on a ring or amulet so they don't have to imprint it many times.

BEST WAY TO FARM LEGENDARY AND UNIQUE ITEMS

In a game this big, there are bound to be one or more ways to farm loot. But since Diablo 4 is a "live service" game, fans can expect such exploits to be fixed quickly if Blizzard thinks they are too bad for the game. So, the next farming method won't use any of those things. Instead, it will focus on farming the way the game's creators meant it to be done.

The best way to get good items in Diablo 4 is to do Public Events on Nightmare difficulty in Helltide areas. Not only are there a lot of Legendaries in the chests from these events, but they also drop Obols and Aberrant Cinders, which can be used to buy even more items.

Things seem to happen more often in Helltide areas, and they also seem to start up again pretty quickly. In some cases, a new event will begin in the same place less than a minute after the last one ended. Before going back to the battlefield, players should stay put or teleport back to town for a while. When they come back, a new event should already be going on.

In Diablo 4, a Grinding event is a very fast way to get all of the Murmuring Obols and Cinders you need from a Greater Radiant Chest. The first one is used to buy things from Curiosity vendors, and the second one is used to open Tortured Gift chests around Helltide. Both of these and the Greater Radiant Chests from events have a chance to give players Legendary and Unique items, but the rate at which Uniques drop on Nightmare mode seems to be very low.

If a Public Event stops showing up in one place, move on to another. Mark one of the spots on the map or keep track of where they are in your head, and keep going back and forth between the two zones until an event happens.

If a zone on the map looks like it's been soaked in blood, it means that a Helltide is happening there right now. If a Helltide is in a place where there are active Grim Whisper bounties, players should start farming there right away to get as much loot as possible.

www.ingramcontent.com/pod-product-compliance
Lightning Source LLC
La Vergne TN
LVHW051332050326
832903LV00031B/3500